Baby Names *for* Boys

Published by :
Lotus Press Publishers & Distributors

Baby Names

for

Boys

Vijaya Kumar

Lotus
PRESS

4735/22, Prakash Deep Building
Ansari Road, Darya Ganj,
New Delhi - 110002

Lotus Press : Publishers & Distributors
Unit No. 220, 2nd Floor, 4735/22, Prakash Deep Building,
Ansari Road, Darya Ganj, New Delhi- 110002
Ph.: 41325510, 23280047, 9811838000
• E-mail : lotuspress1984@gmail.com
www.lotuspress.co.in

Baby Names for Boys

ISBN: 81-8382-122-7

Printed & Published by : **Lotus Press Publisher & Distributors,** New Delhi-02

Choosing Your Baby's Name

Your baby is coming — very great news for you as parents as well as for your parents and everybody in the family — families of both the partners. It may as well be that grand-parents are much more excited than you are, and have already busied themselves with selecting the right name for the soon, arriving little guest, along with other related chores.

So, don't worry any of you because here is a book that provides thousands of names collected from various sources — traditional, new entrants and western as well as now quite favoured Christian and Muslim sources - the world is being truly globalised. And it is okay if your child has a more modern name, because a decade or so hence, when he will grow up, life on the planet will present a totally different shape. And if you prefer traditional names, you are free to do so.

Go ahead and have your choice.

Pronunciation

ā as in *a*rm

ū as in t*oo*

th as in *th*ermal

ṭh as in pat*h* (lesson)

n̄ as in gu*nn* (virtue)

ḍ as in *d*id

ṭ as in *t*ea

A

Aabha: light.

Aabharan: jewel

Aabher: a cowherd.

Aadhunik: modern, new.

Aadi: first.

Aadidev: the first God

Aadinath: the first God

Aaditey: son of Aditi.

Aagyey: unknown.

Aagney: born from fire.

Aahlaadith: Joyous person.

Aahwaanith: who has been invited, wanted.

Aakanksh: desire.

Aakar: form, shape.

Aalam: the whole world.

Aalap: musical prelude, conversation.

Aaliyah: sunshine, happy, bright.

Aandaleeb: bulbul (Bird).

Aanjaney: lord Hanuman.

Aaraadhak: worshipper.

Aarjav: one who is steadfast in happiness or sorrow.

Aashka: receiving or taking blessings from the God.

Aashlesh: to embrace.

Aashrith: ruler

Aastik: one who has faith in God.

Aathiswaran: fhe fire.

Aatish: fire.

Aatma: soul.

Aatmaj: son.

Aayakumar: son of Urvashi an Puroonava son of Sri Krishna and Bhadra.

Aayu: span of life.

Abālendu: full moon.

Abayomi: he who brings joy.

Abbot: father.

Abdar: wealthy, glittering with water.

Abdel: servant.

Abdul: servant.

Abdullah: servant of God

Abe: breath.

Abel: breath, exhalation of breath, the second son of Adam.

Aben: Father of multitudes.

Abhar: shining, brilliant, radiant.

Ābhās: splendour, colour, light, reflection.

Ābhāt: shining, blazing, appearing, visible.

Abhay: fearless, undaunted, Shiva.

Abhayanand: delighting in fearlessness.

Abhayañkar: one who causes safety.

Abhayasimha: as fearless as Lion.

Abheek: fearless, passionate lover.

Abheeshta: ones desire

Abheest: wanted, desired.

Abhi: fearless.

Abhibhāva: powerful, overpowering, victorious.

Abhichandra: with a moon-like face.

Abhideep: illuminated.

Abhigeet: praised in song.

Abhigyan: re-collection.

Abhihit: expression, name, word.

Abhijan: of noble descent, family ornament.

Abhijāt: well-born, fit, handsome, learned, noble, proper, wise.

Abhijay: conquest, total victory.

Abhijin: eighth division of the time of the day.

Abhijit: one who has been conquered, one who has conquered, victorious.

Abhik: beloved.

Abhikām: affection, desire.

Abhikānksh: desire, yearning, wish.

Abhilash: wish, desire, pleasure, yearning.

Abhimaan: one with self-respect.

Abhimand: gladdening.

Abhimāni: full of pride.

Abhimanyu: with self-respect, fiery, heroic.

Abhimod: delight, joy.

Abhināmin: one with a famous name, renowned.

Abhinand: to rejoice, be glad, bless, delight, celebrate glad, desire, wish, pleasure.

Abhinandan: congratulations handsome son.

Abhinandit: delighted, saluted, applauded, made happy.

Abhinav: fresh, new, young, modern.

Abhinavan: innovation.

Abhindra: = Devendra, Indra, King of heavens.

Abhineet: well carried, even-minded, forgiving, patient, kind, friendly, well-performed.

Abhinivesh: long cherished desire, idea, resolution.

Abhinu: brave man.

Abhipāl: protector.

Abhir: red powder used during Holi.

Abhira: cow herd.

Abhiraj: handsome.

Abhirakshit: one who is protected.

Abhirām: pleasing, agreeable, beautiful, delightful, Shiva.

Abhirat: immensed.

Abhirath: great chariotist, Handsome.

Abhirūp: pleasing form, handsome, charming, wise, beautiful, learned, delightful, Vishnu, Shiva, moon.

Abhisār: spreading brightness, companion.

Abhishek: anointing, consecrating, installation of king.

Abhishikt: anointed, enthroned.

Abhisneh: desire, affection.

Abhishok: loving, passionate.

Abhit: undaunted, fearless.

Abhivaadan: salute.

Abhivachan: good word, promise.

Abhivād: reverential salutation.

Abhivadak: one who salutes with respect.

Abhivandan: salute.

Abhivandya: one who is treated respectfully.

Abhiveer: commander.

Abhra: mica, gold, sky, camphor, a cloud.

Abhyuday: sunrise, increase, elevation, good result, happiness, prosperity.

Abhyudit: prosperous, risen.

Abid: ocean, moon.

Abijah: the lord is my father.

Abilash: hope, wish, desire.

Abiyah: god is my father.

Abrad: very cold, leopard.

Abrar: truthful people, saints.

Abruk: blessed one.

Abu: father, lotus, waterlily, lord, master.

Abyan: pure, clean.

Abyāz: white.

Abzar: powerful, strong, mighty.

Achal: immovable, rock, mountain.

Achálendra: lord of the immovable, lord of the mountains.

Achalraj: Himalayan mountain.

Acchindra: flawless, perfect, uninterrupted.

Acheer: early.

Achin: without worries.

Achintya: inconceivable, a name of Lord Shiva God.

Achyut: firm, solid, immovable, imperishable.

Achyutanand: the almighty.

Adair: from the oak tree ford.

Adalard: brave and noble.

Adar: fiery.

Ādarsh: ideal, principle, perfection, mirror, new moon day.

Adelik: successful.

Ādesh: command, order, instruction, advice, precept.

Adhār: foundation, base.

Adheer: restless.

Adheesh: lord, master.

Adheet: learned, meditated upon.

Adhij: superior by birth.

Adhik: more, superior, elevated, excess.

Adhikshit: lord, ruler.

Adhip: king.

Adhir: Krishna.

Adhirohan: ascending.

Adhish: God, king.

Adhishwar: emperor, supreme authority (The God).

Adhor: Shiva.

Adhvar: careful not to cause injury, sacrifice.

Ādi: beginning, first-born.

Ādikar: first creator, Brahma.

Adil: sincere, just.

Ādim: beginning, origin, root.

Adin: magnificent.

Adinarayan: Vishnu.

Adinath, Aadinath: father of Bharata & Bahubali, leader

Adip: king, leader.

Adipurush: Paramatma.

Adirāj: monarch, emperor.

Adish: commanded, ordered, directed, pointed out, ruler, lord, chief.

Adishankar: Sri Sankaracharya, founder of Adwaitha Philosophy.

Adishesh: serpent God.

Adisura: name of an ancient king, Vishnu.

Ādit: first, sun.

Āditeya: son of Aditi, sun.

Aditi: infinite.

Āditya: belonging to Aditi, sun.

Ādityaketu: sun-bannered.

Ādityanandan: son of the sun.

Ādityasānu: son of the sun.

Aditya Vardhan: one who embellishes the Sun.

Ādityavardhan: increaser of glory.

Ādityavarman: protected by the adityas.

Ādityavarn̄a: colour of the sun.

Ādityesh: lord of the adityas, sun.

Ādivaki: first seen, Brahma.

Adjovi: prince.

Adraksh: lightning.

Adreesh: invisible.

Adrendra: lord of the mountains.

Adri: hard, rock, mountain, cloud, sun, thunderbolt.

Adrij: belonging to mountains.

Adrik: bold.

Adrup: consuming the earth.

Adunni: a child that everyone would like to have.

Ad ūr: not far, near, omnipresent, soul.

Adūshit: unspotted, irreproachable, guileless.

Advaid: a sage.

Advait: having no duplicate, unique, sole.

Advaita: non-duality.

Advay: without a second, unique, non-believer of duality.

Advayānand: absolute bliss.

Advik: unique.

Adviteeya: unique, without a second, matchless.

Adwin: artist.

Adwithiya: without a second, unequalled peerless.

Adyot: enveloped by light, brilliant.

Afam: loyal.

Afrāah: happiness, joy.

Afrāz: height, elevation.

Aftab: the Sun.

Agādhi: deep, unfathomable.

Āgam: emerging, birth, wisdom, knowledge.

Agarkar: surname.

Agarva: free from pride.

Agasti: name of a sage

Agastya: name of a saint, name of a sage, name of a star.

Agavāh: born of a fire, borne by a mountain, lord of sacrifices, offerings showered into the sacred fire.

Agendra: lord of the mountains.

Agha: master, lord, chief, elder brother, mister, another name for god.

Aghad: vast, deep, unfathomable the God.

Aghamanshan̄: destroying sin.

Agharna: the moon

Aghor: gentle nature of shiva, one of the five faces of shiva.

Aghoranath: Shiva.

Aghosh: quiet, soundless.

Agira: sun, fire.

Agnajit: conquerer of fire.

Āgneedhra: descendant of fire.

Agneya: direction owned by Agni, the direction between east and south.

Āgney: son of Agni.

Agnibh: radiant like fire, gold.

Agnibhatta: as noble as fire, Agni.

Agnibhū: born of fire.

Agnidatta: given by fire, given to the fire.

Āgnidhrak: descendant of fire.

Agnihamsa: athma, soul.

Agnij: born of fire, gold, Vishnu.

Āgnijwal: flame of fire, Shiva.

Āgnik: born of fire.

Agnikañ: spark of fire, particle of fire.

Agniketu: fire-bannered, with fire as the main characteristic.

Agnikumār: son of Agni.

Agnim: torch bearer, leader, elder brother.

Agnimash: stinging like fire.

Agnimitra: friend of fire.

Agnirājan: glorified by fire, with Agni as king.

Agnisambhav: born of fire.

Agnishikh: fire-crested, flame of fire, lamp, arrow, pointed.

Agnisom: fire and nectar conjoined.

Agnishree: with the brightness of fire.

Agnishtu: devotee of fire.

Agniswāmin: lord of fire.

Agnivesh: name of a saint, an ancient medical authority.

Agnitejas: with fire lustre, with fire energy.

Agnivallabh: beloved of the fire.

Agnivarña: fire-coloured, hot, fiery, red-faced.

Agniveerya: with the power of fire, god.

Agnivesh: fire-clad, as glorious as fire.

Agniveshya: eneveloped by fire, offerer of oblation.

Agrahar: a plot of land given to a Brahman by a king.

Agraj: born first, eldest.

Āgrayaṅ: leader, offering of first fruit, a form of fire.

Agreni: first, leader, preceding.

Agrim: advance, first.

Agrima: leadership.

Agriya: first, best.

Agyey: unknown.

Ahab: uncle.

Ahalad: enjoy.

Ahamyāt: egoless.

Ahan: dawn, morning.

Ahankār: causer of day, sun.

Ahanmaṅi: jewel of the day, sun.

Ahannāth: lord of the day, sun.

Ahanpati: lord of the day, sun.

Ahanti: indestructible.

Ahar: defender.

Aharbandhav: friend of the defenders, friend of day, sun.

Aharmaṅi: jewel of the day, sun.

Aharpati: lord of the day, sun, Shiva.

Ahaskar: producing the day.

Aheekā: of heaven and earth, silk cotton tree.

Aheen: all, entire, whole, serpent.

Aheenagu: excellent ray.

Aheendra: lord of serpents.

Ahern: lord of horses.

Ahi: sun, cloud, water, number, serpent.

Ahidhar: who wears serpents, Shiva.

Ahijeet: conqueror of the serpent, Krishna, Indra.

Ahilochan: serpent-eyed.

Ahim: not cold, hot, cloud, water, traveller.

Ahimakar: hot-rayed, cloud, water, traveller.

Ahirath: having a snake chariot.

Āhlād: causing delight, refreshing.

Ahladith: joyous person.

Ahren: eagle.

Ahsan: obligation.

Ahupati: follower of prayer, a devotee.

Āhut: invited, invoked, called, summoned.

Āhvān: invocation.

Ahwanith: who has been invited, wanted.

Aidan: fiery.

Aijaz: favour.

Aiken: oaken, sturdy.

Aila: intellect-born.

Ainesh: the suṇs glory.

Airavat: as fast as the wind.

Aitareya: unique.

Ajā: not born, self-existent, eternal, leader of a flock, ram, driver, Brahma, Vishnu, Shiva.

Ajaata: unborn.

Ajabu: rare.

Ajaikapāl: herdsman, protector of cattle, lord of animals.

Ajakāv: bow of the unborn.

Ajānidh: treasure or ocean of instigation.

Ajar: ageless, God.

Ajarā: ever young, Saraswati.

Ajasra: not to be obstructed.

Ajāt: unborn, a god.

Ajātari: having no enemy.

Ajatashatru: without enemies.

Ajathashathru: one who has enemies.

Ajavindu: with knowledge of eternity.

Ajax: eagle.

Ajay: unconquerable, invincible.

Ajeesh: lords of goats, Shiva.

Ajina: tigerskin, goatskin.

Ajinkya: invincible.

Ajir: fast, agile, rapid.

Ajit: invincible irresistable, Vishnu, Shiva.

Ajitābh: unconquerable brilliance.

Ajitesh: unconquerable.

Ajitnāth: lord of the invincible.

Ajitpāl: protector of the invincible.

Ajitāman: unconquerable soul, pious, pure, chaste.

Ajmal: pious.

Ajur: ever young.

Akalañk: stainless, flawless, unblemished.

Akalmāsh: sinless.

Akalpa: ornament, decoration.

Akalush: unblemished.

Akām: lustless, chaste, pious, virtuous.

Ākampan: calm, unshaken, resolute.

Akampit: unshaken, calm, resolute.

Akansh: hope, desire.

Akañṭak: free from thorns, without enemies or troubles.

Akapivat: unshaken, firm, tranquil, resolute.

Akarshak: attravtive.

Ākarshañ: attraction, charming, handsome.

Ākarshit: attracted, admirer of beauty.

Ākash: touchstone.

Ākāsh: free or open space, ether, sky, open-minded, atmosphere, one whose thoughts pervade the sky.

Akashaling: Shivaling at Chidambaram.

Ākāshdeep: lamp in the sky.

Akath: boisterous.

Akbar: very big, very great.

Akeno: bright shining field.

Ākhanḍ: that which cannot be broken, Shiva.

Akhandanand: fully happy.

Akhat: safe, unharmed.

Akhil: complete, whole.

Akhilātman: universal soul.

Akhilendra: lord of the universe.

Akhilesh: all-pervading god.

Akhileshwar: supreme being.

Akhtar: star omen.

Akhyath: famous.

Akil: intelligent.

Akilandeshwar: lord of the world, god, king, emperor.

Akili: wiseone.

Aklank: innocent.

Akmal: complete.

Akop: calmone of the Ministers of Dasharatha

Akram: excellent.

Akrānt: unsurpassed. unconquered.

Ākriti: form, shape.

Ākrodhan: free from anger.

Akroor: gentle, Krishnąs friend, a Yadava chief.

Akrūr: not cruel, gentle.

Aksh: soul, knowledge, earth, sky, senses.

Akshaj: diamond, lightning.

Akshan: eye.

Akshapad: Gautam.

Akshar: eternal, imperishable, wood.

Akshat: uninjured, unscathed, whole, Vishnu.

Akshayakeerthi: eternal fame.

Akshay Keerti: eternal fame.

Akshay: direct knowledge, diamond, thunderbolt, Vishnu.

Akshak: sensual, chariot tree.

Akshakum ār: eternal prince.

Akshalā: unbroken, whole, Shiva.

Akshamat: rosary, string of beads with Rudraksh beads.

Akshapād: follower of knowledge, learned, wise, enlightened.

Akshar: imperishable, unchangeable, Brahma, Vishnu, Shiva, syllable Om, final beatitude.

Akshat: unbroken, whole, Shiva.

Akshay: imperishable, undecaying, Supreme Spirit.

Akshin: not perishing, non-waning, non-diminishing.

Akshit: undecaying, eternal, unfailing.

Akshitavās: having undecaying wealth.

Akshobhya: immovable, unassailable, unperturbed.

Akshudra: big or important, Shiva.

Aktar: scent, fragrance.

Aktu: ray, light, tinge.

Akul: transcendental, without caste, without family, Shiva.

Akunṭha: vigorous, eternal, always fresh.

Akūpār: unbounded, free, independent, ocean.

Akūrcha: guileless one.

Akush: lap.

Akutil: upright, straight forward.

Akyās: wise, intelligent.

Alagesh: lord of individuals.

Alap: conversation, development of a tune before the song is sung.

Alak: lock of curly hair.

Alaka: capital of Kuber dynasty.

Alakananda: river.

Alakshya: visible, apparent.

Alam: the whole world.

Alambal: with immeasurable power.

Ālambi: dependable.

Alamgir: the lord of the whole world.

Alan: handsome.

Alanis: attractive, peaceful, rock, full of cheer, fair, handsome.

Alankār: ornament.

Alankrit: adorned, decorated.

Alankriti: ornament.

Alap: conversation, development of a tune before the song is sung.

Alasdair: variant of Alexander.

Alastair: defender of mankind, strong.

Alcott: old cottage.

Aleeh: idol.

Aleem: a learned person, knowledgeable.

Alek: form of Alexander, defender of Mankind.

Alesh: much, large.

Alfred: wise counsel.

Alkādip: lord of the Alaka city.

Alhad: joy.

Ali: protected by god, the highest, the greatest.

Alif: familiar, itimate, tame, friend, geneial, associate, companion, beloved.

Alipth: neutral, dispassionate, detached.

Alman: a kind of Song.

Alobhin: free from greed, not desiring anything.

Ālok: vision, aspect, light, lustre, sight, splendour.

Alol: unagitated, calm, steady, firm.

Alon: oak tree.

Ālop: a small bit.

Alpasāras: a little jewel.

Alpesh: subtle god, Krishna.

Altaf: kindness, grace, favours, gifts, courtesy.

Altair: first magnitude star in the constellation Aquilla.

Altman: oldman.

Āluk: ebony.

Alva: sublime.

Alvin: elf, wine, noble friend, loved by All.

Alvis: all knowing.

Alya: apt.

Amad: without intoxication, grave, sober, serious.

Amadan: opposed to sex, sexless, free of sexual desires, Shiva.

Amadeo: loved by God.

Amadhya: not indifferent compassionate, loving, humane, Krishna.

Amal: spotless, clean, crystal, pure, shining, Vishnu.

Amalanand: pure joy.

Amalātman: pure-minded, pure, chaste, virtuous.

Amalendu: moon.

Amalesh: pure.

Āman: affection, kindness, amicable, friendly.

Aman: peace, tranquillity.

Amānath: property, treasure, extremely wealthy.

Amand: not slow, active, bright, merry.

Amanda: worthy of love.

Amandeep: sharp-witted, light of peace, lamp of peace.

Am ānush: non-human, divine, celestial, demonic.

Amar: immortal, imperishable, Rudraksh tree.

Amara: eternally beautiful, immortal.

Amarabahu: son of Anaranya of Ecchvaku dynasty.

Amarādhip: lord of the gods, Shiva.

Amaraj: eternally born, of eternal existence.

Amarakeerthi: eternal fame.

Amarchandra: moon among gods, immortal moon.

Amarchit: unsubdued.

Amardatta: given by the gods.

Amareesh: lord of the gods.

Amarejya: preceptor of the gods.

Amarendra: king of devas, Devendra.

Amaresh: king of Devas, Devendra, person who never dies, immortal.

Amarjeet: conquering the gods.

Amarjot: light of the gods.

Amarjyoti: eternal light.

Amarnāth: lord of the gods, Shiva.

Amaranjay: conquering the gods.

Amareeshwar: lord of the immortals, Vishnu, Shiva.

Amaresh: lord of the gods, Shiva.

Amarik: deathless immortal, divine.

Amarishnu: desiring immortality.

Amaropam: like a god.

Amarottam: best among gods.

Amarpā: lord of the gods.

Amarpreet: immortal love.

Amarshree: eternally divine, Vishnu, Shiva.

Amarthya: an immortal, a Deva.

Amartya: immortal, divine.

Amaru: immortal.

Amaruk: son of an immortal.

Amarūpam: god-like.

Āmas: fine, raw, soft, teṇder, not gross, not dark.

Amāy: guileless.

Amay: boundless, immeasurable, endless.

Amayātman: with immense power of the mind, Vishnu.

Ambak: eye.

Ambar: sky, atmosphere, ether, circumference, saffron, a kind of perfume.

Ambaramaṇi: jewel of the sky, sun.

Ambareesh: lord of the sky, atmosphere, Vishnu, Shiva, Ganesha.

Ambasth: devotee of the sky, devotee of goddess Amba, water-resider.

Ambav: water-like, sounding like running water.

Ambassār: essence of water, pearl.

Amber: the sky.

Amberam: the sky.

Ambhoj: water-born, lotus.

Ambhriṇ: full of water, powerful.

Ambu: water.

Ambud: the cloud.

Ambudhi: the sea.

Ambuj: water-produced, lotus, Indra's thunderbolt, conch, moon, Indian oak tree.

Ambujabhū: born in a lotus, Brahma.

Ambujanabh: Vishnu.

Ambunāth: lord of the waters, ocean.

Ambunidhi: reservoir of water, ocean.

Amburāj: lord of the waters, ocean.

Ameek: very deep.

Ameen: honest, trust worthy, divine grace.

Ameer: rich.

Ameet: limitless, Vishnu.

Amery: ridge, long hill.

Amey: boundless.

Ameya: immesasurable.

Amichai: my people live.

Amil: invaluable, unconserned.

Amin: faithful, trustworthy, honest.

Amir: prince.

Amish: an object of enjoyment, gift, pleasing object.

Amit: immeasurable, boundless, great, immense, infinite, unlimited.

Amitābh: of unmeasured splendour.

Amitamathi: one of the ministers of Bahubali.

Amitāsan: with sacred marks, omnipresent, Vishnu.

Amitātman: with an immense mind.

Amitav: limitless lusture.

Amitava: same as Amitabh.

Amitavikram: of unlimited valour, Vishnu.

Amitay: boundless.

Amitāyush: of infinite age, immortal, divine.

Amitesh: lord of the infinite, Vishnu.

Amitosh: ever happy.

Amitrasudan: destroyer of enemies.

Amiy: nectar.

Amiya: imperishable.

Amjad: more glorious, worshipable.

Amlan: unfading, everbright.

Amlān: unwithered, fresh, bright, clean, dear, unclouded.

Amod: happiness.

Āmod: amusement, cheer, gladness, joy, strong, perfume, pleasure, serenity.

Āmodin: fragrant, famous.

Amodine: joyful.

Amogh: unerring, fruitful, productive, unfailing.

Amoghadarshan: with an unerring eye.

Amoghavarsha: king.

Amoghsiddi: one who does not fall.

Amoh: without delusion, errorless, clear, straight.

Amol: priceless, invaluable.

Amolak: priceless.

Amolik: priceless.

Amon: hidden.

Amory: brave, powerful.

Amram: a mighty nation.

Amrik: nectar.

Amrit: immortal nectar, ambrosia, Supreme Spirit, anything sweet, beautiful, God, gold, light, ray of the sun, splendour, Vishnu, Shiva.

Amritaharaṇ: stealer of nectar, moon.

Amritak: nectar of immortality.

Amritākshar: imperishable.

Amritānand: delight of immortals.

Amritānshu: nectar-rayed, moon.

Amritāsh: immortal soul, nectar-drinker, Vishnu.

Amritesh: lord of the immortals, Shiva.

Amriteshay: sleeping in nectar, Vishnu.

Amritodan: cloud of nectar.

Amruth: nectar, food of devas.

Amruthamshu: the moon

Amruthasagar: sea of nectar, full of sweetness.

Amshumalin: the sun.

Amteshwar: eternal God, immortal, virtuous.

Amūl: without a beginning, rootless, without a superior, one who does not have anyone to follow.

Amūlya: invaluable.

Amūrā: wise, intelligent, sharp-eyed.

Amurog: affection, love, redness.

Amūrta: formless, Shiva.

Amūrti: formless, all-prevading, omnipresent, Vishnu.

Amzad: worshipable.

Anaadhi: without beginning.

Anadaram: Sri Ram.

Anādinav: faultless, without a beginning, forever new.

Anādya: existing from eternity. Krishna.

Anādyant: with no beginning or end, eternal, immortal, divine, Shiva.

Anagh: sinless, pure, innocent, perfect, above reproach, Vishnu, Shiva.

Anagha: sinless.

Anak: without weakness, thundercloud.

Anākrānt: unassailable, invincible, strong, victorious.

Anal: fire, wind.

Analaksha: Shiva.

Analjit: conqueror of fire, blameless, invincible, pure.

Anam: acknowledger of salutations with blessings.

Anāmay: free of disease, healthy, Shiva.

Anamitra: without any enemy, liked by all, Yadava chief head of Indian Virshini among Yadavas.

Anamiv: free of disease, happy, well.

Anandmoorti: happiness personified.

Angshu: ray of light.

Angus: unique choice, singular.

Anik: soldier

Anilaabh: zephyr.

Anmol: priceless, precious, rare.

Ānan: face, appearance.

Ananat: proud, upright, undefeated.

Ānand: happy, bliss, enjoyment, pleasure, joy, Shiva.

Ānandātman: whose essence is happiness, whose soul is blissful, whose soul has attained salvation.

Anandavardhan: one who increases happiness.

Ānandgiri: peak of joy, bringer of joy, one full of joy.

Ānandmohan: delightful, Krishna.

Ānandsāgar: sea of joy.

Ānadhik: having no superior.

Anandi: eternal, primordial the God.

Ānandin: blissful, cheerful, happy.

Ānandit: blissful, delighted, happy.

Anang: formless, limbless, divine, corporeal, Arabian jasmine, Cupid God of Love.

Ananga: Kamadeva.

Anangam: beyond body, beyond passion, beyond destruction, divine, air, ether, mind, sky.

Anangapāl: protector of the limbless, protector of the gods, divine, immortal, spiritual, religious.

Ananjan: without collyrium, faultless, taintless, sky, Supreme Spirit, Vishnu.

Ananmay: one who cannot be broken, healthy, Vishnu.

Anant: endless, sky, cloud, beyond death, imortal, divine, eternal, Vishnu, Brahma, Shiva, Krishna, Supreme Spirit.

Ananta: infinite.

Anantadev: immortal deity.

Anantagun̄: with infinite virtues.

Anantajeet: ever victorious.

Anantanāth: eternal lord, eternal, divine, Vishnu.

Anantarām: ever pleasing.

Anantarūp: innumerable forms, Vishnu.

Anantashakti: of boundless power, Supreme Spirit.

Anantashayan: supine on serpent Shesha, Vishnu.

Anantashree: of limitless magnificence, Supreme Being.

Anantavarman: with supreme power, Supreme Being.

Anantavikram: with eternal valour.

Ānantya: endless, eternal, divine.

Anarañya: possessor of eternal power.

Anargha: priceless.

Anāsh: indestructible undivided, sky, Supreme Being.

Anāshay: without self-interest, selfless.

Anāshin: indestructible, imperishable.

Anāsh: imperishable, indestructible.

Anasūri: not unwise, active, alert, energetic, intelligent.

Anashwar: imperishable.

Anashya: indestructible.

Anav: humane, kind to men.

Anchal: piece of cloth worn round the waist by ascetics.

Andesh: meditation.

Aneek: army, brilliance, face, front, form, splendour.

Aneel: not blue, fair.

Aneelābh: not blue, bright, fair, shining, white, zephyr.

Aneesh: without a superior, supreme, paramount, Vishnu.

Aneeshvar: without a superior, paramount.

Anekalochan: with several eyes, all-seeing, always, Shiva.

Anenas: blameless, sinless.

Anenasya: freedom from sin, chaste, pure, pious.

Angad: bestower of limbs, with beautiful limbs, armlet, powerful.

Angaj: body-produced, son, immortal love.

Angak: son.

Angam: impierceable.

Anganemi: follower of the scriptures.

Angrāj: most handsome.

Angiras: knower of *Vedas*, knower of the scriptures.

Angoshin: resonant, praiseworthy.

Angshu: with beautiful limbs.

Angus: superb, unique.

Āngush: praising hymn.

Aniket: homeless, to whom the entire world is his home.

Anil: wind, god of wind, Vishnu, Shiva.

Anilaabh: Zephyr.

Anilātmaj: son of the wind, strong, swift.

Anilkumar: son of wind (Hanuman).

Animān: immense, unlimited, beyond boundary.

Animesh: alert, vigilant, unwinking, Vishnu.

Animish: a Deva.

Anin: small.

Aṇindat: one who does not speak ill of others, one who is not spoken ill of.

Anindit: blameless.

Aniran: eternal flame.

Anirbān: unextinguished, immortal, eternal.

Anirjit: unconquered.

Anirvan: deathless, god, undying.

Aniruddha: unopposed, unobstructed.

Anirudh: which cannot be restricted.

Anirvin̄: not tired or downcast, active, energetic progressive.

Anish: god Vishnu.

Anitej: of immeasurable splendour.

Anivartin: does not retreat, brave, Vishnu, Supreme Being.

Anjaana: stranger.

Anjuman: a token, a symbol, a signet.

Anjak: decorated, anointed.

Anjal: hollow formed by joining two hand, worship, A way of welcoming by Indians.

Anjalik: bearer of arrows.

Anjan: collyrium, grey in complexion.

Anjaneya: Hanuman, son of Anjana.

Anjani: innocent. Hanuman.

Anjanikumar: lord Hanuman, son of Anjana Devi.

Anjas: guileless, honest, straightforward.

Anjik: blessed, black, dark.

Anjishn̄u: dispeller of darkness, very brilliant, sun.

Anjuli: revered, worshipped.

Anjuman: a token, a symbol, a signet.

Anjum: a token, star.

Anjun: collyrium.

Ankalesh: God.

Ankati: wind, fire.

Ankit: marked.

Ankolik: accepted, respected, loved, embraced.

Ankūr: sprout, newborn, blade, short.

Ankush: check, an instrument used for guiding elephants, instrument used to control the Elephant.

Anmol: invaluable.

Annad: granter of food, Shiva.

Anoon: flawless, perfect.

Anoop: place full of water.

Ansal: strong, lusty.

Ansejal: wandering angel

Ansh: part, day, share, a part of something.

Anshak: an heir.

Anshal: heir.

Ansharin: heir.

Anshin: heir.

Anshu: ray, minute particle, sunbeam, beam of light, lustre, splendour, brilliance, speed.

Anshubān: with rays for arrows, sun.

Anshudhar: bearer of rays, sun.

Anshujal: a gathering of rays, a blaze of light, enlightening, brilliant, illuminating.

Anshuk: leaf, ray, bright, enlightening, bright, illuminating.

Anshul: luminous, radiant, bright, enlightening.

Anshumāl: garland of rays, halo, as brilliant as the sun.

Anshumālin: garlanded with rays, sun.

Anshumān: having rays, sun, moon, radiant, enlightening, illuminating.

Anshumat: one with rays, sun, moon, radiant, luminous.

Anshuvān: with rays as arrows, sun.

Antam: without darkness, nearest, next, intimate.

Antang: a complete person.

Antar: near, heart, soul, guarantee, related, intimate, interior.

Antaresh: name of a giant red star.

Antariksh: outer space, sky.

Antarip: island.

Antarjyotish: with an illumined soul.

Anthahkaran: kindness, sympathy, fellow feeling, tenderness.

Antosha: inestimable.

Āntya: accomphisher.

Ānu: being, human, living.

Anu: follower.

Aṅu: atom, minute, divine, subtle, Shiva.

Anubhav: experience, perception.

Anubhuti: experience, feeling.

Anubodh: after-thought, recollection.

Anuchān: well versed in the *Vedas*, devoted to learning.

Anuchand: handsome.

Anudeep: lamp.

Anudeshya: obedient, goal-proceeder.

Anudrutta: with subtle movement, all-pervading divine, swift.

Anugāyas: praised in hymn.

Anugra: gentle, peaceful, mild.

Anugraha: favour, benevolence, Vishnu.

Anugun: fitting.

Anuhlad: brother of Prahlad.

Anuj: born later, younger brother.

Anukarsh: invoking, summoning.

Anukāsh: reflection of light.

Anukrosh: gentle, tender, compassionate.

Anukūl: agreeable, amicable, favourably disposed.

Anumit: analytical, precise.

Anumodan: pleasing, causing delight.

Anunay: gentle comfort, supplication, consolation.

Anūp: unequalled, unique, abounding in water.

Anupam: incomparable, matchless, rare, precious, ginger.

Anupati: lord of the atom, lord of the subtle.

Anupradān: gift, donation.

Anūpya: matchless, unique, incomparable.

Anurādh: bestower of happiness.

Anurāg: affection, attachment, love, passion, red.

Anurāgin: love-inducer.

Anurāj: brilliant, enlightening, illuminating.

Anuranjan: satisfying, pleaser, attachment-inducer, one who is loved.

Anuranjit; pacified, satisfied, reconciled.

Anurodh: request.

Anurūp: agreeable, compatible, suitable, in shape, follower of form.

Anush: following desires, seeking desires.

Anushik: crested, adorned, embellished, respected, decorated.

Anushobhin: shining, dignified, glorious, graceful, enlightening, illuminating, bright.

Anushrut: well-known, handed down by Vedic tradition

Anutosh: relief, gratification.

Anutta: unconquerable.

Anuttam: having no superior, supreme, best, highest, unsurpassed, Vishnu, Shiva.

Anuva: new beginning.

Anuvas: to make fragrant.

Anuvind: discoverer or obtainer, striver of success.

Anuvrat: devoted, loyal, faithful, attached.

Anveshak: one who persues, seeker.

Anveshan: finding.

Anwar: devotee of God.

Anyanga: spotless, pure, pious, flawless, virtuous.

Anyūn: healthy, without defect, entire, whole, complete, total.

Apachit: honoured, repected.

Apah: sun, brilliant, radiant, glorious, enlightening, illuminating.

Apalāshin: free from desire.

Apamanyu: free from grief.

Apar: limitless, great, God.

Aparāditya: like the sun, brilliant, radiant.

Aparājit: undefeated, unsurpassed, Vishnu, Shiva.

Aparajito: undefeated.

Aparampar: limitless.

Apariman: immeasurable, immense, unbounded.

Aparimey: unmeasurable, immense, unlimited, unbounded.

Aparimat: unlimited, immense, unbounded.

Apareet: irresistable.

Āpareet: joyous, gladdened.

Aparoop: uncommon, rare.

Aparñesh: lord of Parvati, Shiva.

Aparoksh: not beyond sight, visible, manifest.

Apārthiv: divine, subtle, immortal.

Aparush: without anger.

Apashank: fearless.

Apaspati: active, skilful.

Apasya: active, skilful.

Āpav: wind-sheltered, grove.

Apekshit: desired.

Apiguñ: with attributes, excellent, virtuous.

Apij: born after, born in addition to, brother.

Apeendra: resembling Indra, handsome, divine, virtuous.

Apnavān: support provider.

Apod: another name of sage Doumya.

Apoorva prakash: matchless glow,

Aprameya: beyond comprehension God.

Appit: fire.

Aprajay: invincibility.

Aprakarshit: undiminished, unequalled, irresistable.

Apramay: eternal, imperishable.

Aprameya: beyond comprehension God.

Aprati: without opponents, unequalled irresistable.

Apratihat: without a match.

Apratim: incomparable, supreme.

Apratin: without comparison, unequalled, irresistable.

Aprateep: not adamant, flexible, compromising, adaptive.

Apratirūp: with matchless beauty.

Apratul: unparalleled, unique, uncomparable.

Āpta: goal-achiever, reliable, logical, organised.

Aptu: small, tender.

Apūp: little, honeycomb, cake.

Apurva = unique.

Apūrva: singular, unprecedented, Supreme Soul.

Āpyas: belonging to the water.

Arabhaṭ: brave, enterprising.

Arabinda: lotus.

Ārādhak: worshipper.

Arādhan: adoration, worship.

Arāg: passionless, cool, calm.

Ārāgam: helpful.

Aram: high, exalter, the Hebrew name of ancient Syria.

Aramanas: desire, delight, enjoyment, obedience, pleasure.

Araṅ: distant, heaven.

Aranāth: controller of time.

Araṅis: turning around, sun.

Araṅya: forest, foreign place, desert.

Aravindaksha: lotus eyed, Vishnu.

Aranyak: name of a King.

Araṅyakumār: prince of the forest.

Arav: peaceful.

Aravind: lotus, auspicious, beautiful, fragrant, dear to the gods.

Archā: shining, brilliant, venerated, adored, worshipped.

Archak: worshipper.

Archan: worship, adoration.

Archat: brilliant, shining, glorious, praising.

Archi: flame, ray, prayer-offerer, one to whom prayers are offered.

Archie: valuable, bold.

Ārchik: one who prays.

Archin: shining, religious.

Archishmat; brilliant, flaming, resplendent.

Archit: worshipped.

Ardhendu: crescent moon.

Ardon: bronze, lofty, eager.

Ārdra: soft, tender, warm, young, green, moist, succulent.

Areṅu: pure, dustless, celestial.

Arganjan: act of offering, sacred, pious, venerated.

Argeshwar: lord of offering, Shiva.

Arghya: offering to the lord.

Arha: deserving, Shiva.

Arhan: worshipped, honoured, venerated.

Arhant: worthy, peaceful, mild, gentle, kind, humane, Shiva.

Arhat: deserving, worthy, respectable.

Ari: lion, eagle, the best.

Aric: rule with mercy.

Aridam: destroyer of foes.

Arihan: slayer of enemies.

Arihant: destroyer of enemies, enemy killer.

Arijit: conqueror of enemies, son of Sri Krishna and Bhadra.

Arimejay: conqueror of enemies.

Arindam: destroyer of enemies.

Arinjay: conqueror of enemies, son of Sri Krishna and Bhadra.

Arishṭ: safe, unhurt, secure, neem tree

Arisia: silent vigil

Arisudan: enemy killer.

Ārit: praised.

Arjan: conqueror of enemies.

Ārjav: upright, straight, honest, sincere.

Arjit: acquired, earned, gained.

Arjun: made of silver, peacock, white, bright, clear, dawn, milk, lightning, fair-minded, pure, glorious, radiant, enlightening.

Arka: ray, sun, fire, flash of lightning, crystal, hymn, scholar, elder brother, red sandalwood tree.

Arkaj: born of the sun.

Arkanandan: son of the sun.

Arkaprakāsh: light of the sun, as bright as the sun.

Arkapriya: beloved of the sun, hibiscus.

Arkash: illumined by the sun, visible, manifest.

Arkesh: the sun.

Arkeshwar: the sun.

Arkin: radiant with light, shining, bright, worshipped, lauded.

Arland: pledge.

Arlen: pledge.

Arlo: strong, manly.

Armān: wish, longing.

Armand: warrior.

Armando: army man.

Armesh: lord of the Sea.

Armon: high place.

Arnan: quick, joyful, torrent valley.

Arṇav: ocean, sea, stream, wave, flood, sun, air.

Arne: eagle.

Arnesh: lord of the sea, the sea.

Arni: high, an ancestor of Jesus.

Arnie: eagle.

Arnon: rushing stream.

Ārochan: bright, radiant, shining.

Ārohan: to rise.

Arpachan: surrendering oneself.

Arpan: sacrifice, give away.

Arpit: dedicated.

Arsha: sky, heaven, of sacred descent, heavenly, divine, venerated.

Arshad: pious.

Arshan: righteous.

Arshat: Jain, ancient.

Arshia: heavenly.

Arshya: heavenly, celestial, of sacred descent.

Arte: noble, bear man.

Arth: meaning, wealth, half.

Arthadarshin: knower of the meaning, knower of the essence, salvation-attainer.

Artham: fortune, golden lotus.

Arthvān: possession of wealth.

Arthur: noble.

Arudra: gentle, kind, soft, calm, tender.

Aruj: healthy.

Arujas: free from.

Arul: shining like the sun, brilliant, enlightening, glorious.

Aruṇ: gold, red, tawny, ruddy, saffron, dawn.

Arunābh: red glow of the sun, life-giving, passionate.

Aruṅachis: rising sun with a red glow.

Aruṅaditya: crimson sun.

Aruṅajyotish: as bright as the sun, Shiva.

Aruṅakamal: red lotus, passionate, famous, fragrant, dear to the gods.

Arunakant: person shining like morning sun.

Arunakanth: person shining like morning sun.

Aruṅākar: red-rayed, sun.

Arunakiran: person shining like sun rays.

Arunamshu: reddish rays.

Aruṅānshu: with red rays.

Arunank: sun.

Arunapallav: rising sun.

Aruṅāv: red flavour, well-preserved, immensely protected.

Aruṅesh: sun.

Aruni: Bramhạ's son, name of a devoted pupil.

Aruṅoday: dawn, blooming, awakened.

Arunodaya: the early dawn.

Arunshu: healing wounds.

Arush: without anger, calm, bright, red, shining, sun.

Arvāchin: favourable.

Arvad: wanderer

Arvan: swift, quick, agile, fast like a horse, fleet-footed.

Arvin: friend of the people, The peoples friend.

Arvind: lotus.

Arvindra: lord of wheels, lord of horses, lord of priests.

Arvud: priest of hymns.

Ārya: honoured, auspicious, attached, dear, devoted, excellent, faithful, kind, masterly, noble, respectable, wise.

Āryachetas: noble-minded.

TĀryadev: lord of the honoured, noble.

Āryak: honourable, respectable.

Āryakumār: noble prince, virtuous, meritorious.

Aryama: sun.

Āryaman: amīdst nobles, noble lineage, belonging to the sun.

Āryamik: noble, virtuous.

Āryamishra: distinguished among nobles.

Aryamitra: a friend of good people.

Āryannam: nature-lover, forest-dweller.

Āryashūr: bravest among the braves, honourable.

Āryendra: lord of the masters.

Āryik: masterly, honoured.

Asa: healer, physician, name of the 3rd king of Judah.

Asamāti: unique, unparalled, unequalled, divine, supreme.

Āsang: attached, devoted, of a loving nature.

Asangas: free from worldly ties, flag, vessel, unobstructed, sharp, soul, independant.

Asav: essence.

Aseem: endless, limitless.

Aseeman: limitless, unbounded, immense, divine.

Aseer: energetic, pious.

Āseet: steady-mindedness.

Asgar: devotee.

Ashamber: the sky, the universe, Shiva, Vishnu, Jina.

Ashan: rock, sky, strong and subtle.

Ashanis: flash of lightning, thunderbolt.

Ashank: doubtless, fearless, certain.

Ashankit: without doubt, clear, fearless, hopeful.

Ashankith: symbol of hope, full of hope, without doubt fear, hesitation.

Āshapurña: fulfilling desires.

Ashatrus: with no foes, moon.

Ashavāh: borne by space, celestial, heavenly, divine.

Ashay: desire, hope, wish.

Ashechan: charming, lovely.

Asher: fortunate, happy, happiness, 8th son of Jacob.

Ashesh: without any residue, whole, entire, perfect, divine, complete.

Ashik: lover.

Āshir: consuming all, fragrant root, fire, sun, wind, diamond.

Ashirvad: blessings, grace.

Ashis: benediction.

Āshish: blessed, venerated, rare, highly sought.

Āshisṭh: very quick, fast, agile, active, rapid.

Ashit: dark.

Ashla: meadow of ash trees.

Āshleshā: embrace, hug.

Ashlynn: meadow of ash trees.

Ashma: stone-hard, cloud, sky, strong, yet subtle.

Ashmak: stone, rock, gem, sky, cloud, thunderbolt.

Āshman: gem, rock, stone, cloud, mountain, thunderbolt.

Ashmant: fireplace.

Ashmit: rock-born, very hard, strong, tough.

Ashmuṇḍ: existing, shining.

Ashok: cheerful, tranqūil, name of the ancient famous king, name of a tree without sorrow.

Ashokā: sorrowless, Ashok tree blossom.

Ashokadatta: given without sorrow, given with happiness.

Ashokakar: sorrow-eliminator.

Ashokavardhan: increasing grieflessness.

Āshpad: seat, authority, power, dignity.

Ashraf: without grief.

Ashrav: obdient, heeding, compliant.

Āshravya: famous, of whom people listen to with interest.

Ashray: = shelter, protection.

Ashraydat: one who gives shelter and protection.

Ashrey: shetter.

Ashrit: invincible, gold.

Āshrit: dependant.

Āshrut: well-known, famous.

Ashtik: believer in God.

Āshu: fast, active, agile, quick.

Āshug: fleet-flooted, fast, arrow, sun, wind.

Ashūl: without thorns, without obstructions, peaceful, ever happy.

Āshumat: mentally agile, quick-witted.

Ashur: god of military prowess and empire, chief God of the Assyrians.

Āshutosh: easily pleased, Shiva.

Ashvalāyan: causes breath, revives.

Ashvant: follower of truth.

Ashvarya: marvellous, extraordinary, surprising, miraculous.

Ashwa: horse, strong, swift, materially successful.

Ashwabh: lightening.

Ashwaghosha: a Sanskrit author and poet.

Ashwalayan: son of Vishwamitra.

Ashwapathi: a king of Madra Kingdom, Savitṛis father.

Ashwas: assurance, consolation.

Ashwasan: assurance, consolation.

Ashwasena: son of Takshak, a Naga son of Sri Krishna and Neela.

Ashwashivas: son of sage Athervangiras of Badarikashram.

Ashwat: holy peepal tree.

Ashwatanarayan: lord Vishnu.

Ashwatthama: fiery tempered.

Ashwin: mounted on horseback, cavalier.

Ashwini: one of the constallations

Ashwinikumar: healer of angels(Devas).

Asim: limitless.

Āsit: at rest, tranquil, peaceful, poised.

Asit: dark coloured, blue, black, unbounded.

Asitabh: with unrestrained glory, amidst light.

Asitabharan: dark complexioned.

Asitāng: with a glorious reign.

Asitāshman: blue gem, lapis lazuli.

Asitvaran: dark complexioned.

Asjita: victorious, always victorious.

Asketa: master of will, master of house.

Askhal: firm, steady unshaken.

Aslam: greeting.

Aslesh: embrance.

Asman: the sky.

Asthamurthi: Shiva.

Asthik: one who believes in God, son of Jarathkaru and Manasa Devi.

Asurari: enemy of demons, Krishna.

Astoiven: keeper of the cats.

Aswattama: Dronąs son.

Atal: immoveable.

Atalas: bottomless, one whose depth cannot be measured, Shiva.

Atamaj: son.

Atamas: without darkness, with a clear mind, flawless, sinless, virtuous.

Atandra: free from indolence, alert, active.

Atanu: without body, divine, corporeal, the Cupid.

Ātapan: causing warmth, Shiva.

Ātāpin: radiating heat.

Atas: soul, air, subtle, divine.

Ateendra: beyond the senses, control over senses, pious, chaste.

Ateet: past.

Ateeth: inconceiveable to sense organs, God.

Atharva: another name of God Ganesh, one of the Vedas.

Atherva: sage, son of Angiras.

Athervan: one of the four Vedas.

Athithi: Rama's grandson, guest.

Athilesh: lord of intelligence.

Atibal: very strong, very powerful.

Atibhāv: superior, overcomer of people and situations, overcomer of emotions.

Atibheem: very strong.

Atidatta: to whom a lot has been bestowed, one on whom love and gifts are showered.

Atideva: excelling the gods.

Atidhanvan: runs very fast.

Atif: compassionate, kind.

Atihat: firmly fixed.

Atim: very proud.

Atimānit: highly respected, highly honoured.

Atimānush: more than human, divine, celestial.

Atimanyu: very zealous.

Atimāy: beyond illusion, attainer of salvation.

Atināman: renowned.

Atirath: wealthy, great with means or assets.

Atirūp: very beautiful.

Ātish: fire, sacred, glowing, purifying, resplendent.

Atishay: superiority, excellence, meritorious, pre-eminent, superior.

Atishi: surpasses, excels, full of fire.

Atishring: surpassing the peak, divine, excelling perfection.

Atisvārya: beyond notes.

Atithi: guest.

Ativarchas: very glorious.

Ativishwa: superior to universe, divine, celestial.

Atiyā: to surpass.

Atiyām: very dark, black.

Atkeel: solidly fixed, unwavering in meditation.

Atma: soul.

Ātmabhāv: mind-born, mind-created.

Atmajyoti: light of soul (atma).

Ātmajyoti: self-knowledge, Supreme Spirit.

Atmalingam: Shivalingam.

Ātman: soul, principle of life, Krishna.

Ātmānand: rejoicing in the soul.

Ātmārām: pervading the soul, omnipresent, Supreme Soul.

Atmavan: Vishnu.

Ātmavir: with a mighty soul, salvation-attainer.

Ātmay: blessed with a long life.

Atnu: sun.

Ātreya: container of glory, one who crosses the three worlds.

Atri: devourer, overcomer, prosperous, glorified Shiva.

Atul: unequalled.

Atulya: matchless, unequalled.

Atur: fragrance of flower.

Atyāditya: surpassing the sun, more than the sun's lustre, glorious, enlightened, renowned.

Atyānand: great joy.

Ātyaztik: endless, infinite, universal.

Augustus: exalted.

Aum: good.

Avabhāsit: shining, bright.

Avabhod: awakening, enlightened, knowledge, perception, wise.

Avachūda: pendant, embellisher, ornaments, pure, of white splendour.

Avadesh: invulnerable king, king Dasaratha father of Lord Ram.

Avadh: which cannot be violated, one who is not vulnerable.

Avajay: overcoming, winning by conquest.

Avajit: won by conquest.

Avajyut: enlightened, illuminator, illumining.

Avakāsh: shining, visible, manifest, space, room, opportunity.

Avalok: who beholds.

Avalokiteshar: Buddha.

Avaneendra: lord of the earth.

Avaneesh: lord of the earth, king.

Avanendra: lord of the earth.

Avani: earth

Avanij: son of the earth, king.

Avanikānt: beloved of the earth, king.

Avanimohan: Sri Krishna.

Avanindra: king of the earth.

Avanipāl: protector of the earth

Avanish: lord of the earth.

Avantas: crest, head ornament, embellishes.

Avaraj: younger brother.

Āvaran: cover, shelter.

Avarokin: brilliant, shining.

Avas: favour, assistance, pleasure, protection.

Avasthya: adaptable, suitable.

Avatsār: presentation.

Avanindra: king of the earth.

Aveechal: firm, resolute.

Avi: favourable air, wind, lord, protector, favourite, kindly disposed, mountain.

Avichai: my father lives.

Avichal: unmovable.

Avidan: father of justice.

Aviel: god is my father.

Avijit: unconquerable.

Avik: living in a group, strength of a diamond.

Avikal: unimpaired, all, whole, perfect, entire.

Aviklav: without confusion, without unsteadiness.

Avilas: without whims, constant, faithful.

Avimukta: harnessed, not free.

Avimuktesh: firm, resolute, Shiva.

Avināsh: undestructible.

Avineesh: a king.

Avindhya: firm, solid, unmoving.

Avirāj: unceasing.

Avirām: continuous, in succession, uninterrupted.

Avirath: continuous.

Avish : poisonless, earth, heaven, river, life-giving, like nectar.

Avishalom: father of peace.

Avishkar: invention.

Avit: protected.

Avitra: protector.

Avkash: leisure, limitless, chance, oppurtunity.

Avlokiteshwara: a Bodhisattva ranked as high as god.

Āvrita: direction, path, method, order.

Avrodhan: one who observes restraint.

Avtar: incarnation.

Avyakta: invisible, not perceptible, Universal Spirit, Vishnu, Shiva.

Avyay: changeless, imperishable, undecaying.

Ayan: motion.

Ayān: nature, temperament.

Ayanda: many.

Ayāsmay: iron.

Ayāsya: valiant, agile, unconquerable.

Ayati: dignity, majesty, spacious.

Ayo: ray of light.

Āyod: life-giver.

Ayodhyanath: Sri Rama.

Ayodhyaram: Sri Rama.

Ayron: exalted on high, Aaron was the brother of Moses

Ayudha: irresistable, unconquerable.

Ayuj: without an equal.

Ayukumar: son of Urvashi an Puroonava son of Sri Krishna and Bhadra.

Āyus: age, life duration, lineage, man, son, family.

Ayush: life.

Āyushmān: blessed with long life.

Āyushtejas: life energy.

Ayut: unimpeded, unbound, myriad.

Ayutājit: conqueror of many.

Azar: ageless, God.

Azeez: friend.

Azhar: ageless. God. famous.

Aziz: famous.

B

Babhri: victorious.

Babhree: fire, tawny, brown, fierce, Vishnu, Shiva, Krishna.

Babhrukesh: with brown hair.

Babil: house, swift.

Bābul: father.

Bachharāj: very strong.

Bachil: one who talks much, orator.

Bādal: cloud.

Baddhānand: pleasure-bound, attached, joyful.

Baddhānurāg: bound by love, feeling affection.

Badridās: devote of Vishnu.

Badrināth: lord of Badri, Vishnu.

Badri Prasad: gift of Badri

Bahaj: joy, rejoicing.

Bahubal: with great strength.

Bahudam: strong, powerful.

Bahudhan: very wealthy.

Bahudhar: diamond, many-edged, Indra's thunderbolt.

Bahugraha: holding much, water jar, receiving much.

Bahugun̄a: with many good qualities.

Bahukalyān̄: well-wisher of many, noble, very illustrious.

Bahukshan̄: enduring much.

Bahul: ample, broad, abundant, large, dense, thick, spacious.

Bahumānya: esteemed, respected by many.

Bahumārgi: follower of many paths, crossroads.

Bahumitra: friend of many, popular, famous.

Bahumūlak: with various origins, many-rooted, obtainer of virtues from many sources.

Bahumūlya: high-priced, precious, rare.

Bahupaṭu: very clever.

Bahuprada: liberal, generous.

Bahupriya: dear to many.

Bahupushpa: with many flowers, decorated with many flowers, respected, venerated.

Bahurai: with great wealth.

Bahūrja: full of energy, strong, energetic, powerful.

Bahushasta: excellent, happy, right.

Bahushrut: extremely learned, well-versed in the *Vedas*, famous.

Bahuvāshin: controller of many.

Bahuvat: strong-armed.

Bahuvid: very learned, enlightened, wise.

Bahuvidh: very intelligent, versatile, talented, many-faceted.

Bahuvikram: very powerful.

Baira: brave.

Bajarang: mighty, powerful.

Bakavat: watchful, tactful, very attentive.

Bakulesh: lord of blossoms.

Bāla: young, simple, pure, sun.

Bālabhril: strong, powerful, mighty.

Bālachandra: crescent moon, young moon, waxing moon.

Bālachārya: behaving like a child, innocent, curious.

Bāladev: young god.

Baladev: lord of strength.

Baladeya: bestower of strength.

Bālāditya: newly risen sun.

Bālagopāl: young cowherd, young Krishna.

Bālagovind: young cowherd, boy Krishna.

Balagupta: protected by strength.

Bālāji: strong, Vishnu.

Balakar: giver of strength, strong supporter.

Bālāki: as innocent as a babe.

Balakrishna: young Lord Krishna.

Balakrit: obtained by power.

Balāksha: strong-eyed.

Balaksha: blameless, innocent, white-hued.

Bālakunḍ: young flower, bud.

Bālamaṇi: small jewel.

Bālamitra: strong friend, friend of the children.

Bālamohan: attracting children, young one who attracts.

Bālamukund: young blossom, soft like a blossom, child.

Balar: strength, power, army.

Balanāth: lord of strength.

Balāngak: strong-limbed, spring season.

Bālānuj: Krishna, younger brother.

Balaprada: bestower of strength.

Bālarāj: lord of the rising sun, lapizlazuli.

Balarāma: abode of strength.

Bālaravi: morning sun.

Bālārka: rising sun.

Bālarun: dawn.

Balashankar: young Lord Shiva

Bālasūrya: rising sun, purple light of dawn, lapiz-lazuli.

Balaswāmi: master of power.

Balaval: very powerful.

Balavān: strong, powerful.

Balavardhan: increasing strength.

Balavarṇin: strong and appearing well.

Balavat: powerful, intense, dense, prevailing.

Balavir: brave, powerful, hero.

Balavrat: worshipping the rising sun.

Balawant: strong.

Bālayogi: young ascetic.

Balayukta: endowed with strength.

Baldev: godlike in power, Balram.

Bālendu: crescent moon, new moon, waxing moon.

Balesh: army commander, lord of power.

Baleshwar: lord of children, Krishna.

Bāli: powerful.

Baliman: powerful.

Balin: powerful, strong, robust, mighty.

Ballalesh: Ganesha.

Ballav: cowherd.

Balochan: Shiva.

Balraj: mighty, powerful.

Balram: lord Krishṇa's brother.

Bālya: child-like, crescent moon.

Bāṇa: arrow, sharp, intellect.

Banavāri: forest dweller, Krishna.

Bancroft: bean field.

Bandana: prayer, chant, sacred, enlightened, illumined, beyond worldly bonds.

Bandin: praiser, bard, heralder.

Baneshwar: lord of the forest.

Bāṇi: speech orator, articulator.

Bāṇibrat: controller of speech, eloquent, orator, devoted to speech.

Bankimchandra: half moon.

Banrender: Shiva.

Banshi: flute, sweet-voiced, melodious.

Banshidhar: bearer of flute, Krishna.

Banshik: king of the forest, lion.

Banshivinod: amuses with flute, Krishna.

Bansi: flute.

Bansilal: lord Krishna.

Bappā: universal father.

Barhaṇ: strong, active, agile, eye-dazzling, energetic, powerful, vigorous.

Barindra: ocean.

Barkhā: rain, life-giving, cool, moistening, soothing.

Barnett: noble man.

Barot: speech.

Barton: from the barley field.

Barū: noble.

Baruṇ: lord of water, found in water.

Basabi: resident.

Basant: spring season.

Bāsav: bull, strong, virile.

Basavarāj: lord of the bulls, extremely strong, very virile.

Basdev: fire.

Bashkal: teacher, preceptor, knower of substance, well-read, enlightened, illumined, wise.

Basil: royal, brave.

Basū: wealthy.

Battu: lad, youth, boy, Shiva.

Baxṭer: baker.

Bayāz: white, bright.

Beant: endless, eternal.

Beejin: cosmic creator, progenitor, sun.

Bekurā: sound, voice, musical instrument, melodious, harmony.

Benson: excellent son.

Beverley: meadow of beavers.

Bhabesh: lord of existence, lord of the universe, lord of emotions.

Bhadra: blessed, auspicious, fair, fortunate, good, happy, handsome, gentlemanly, excellent, gracious, Shiva.

Bhadrak: brave, beautiful, good, handsome, meritorious, virtuous.

Bhadraksh: one with beautiful eyes.

Bhadrasār: essence of goodness, ocean of goodness.

Bhadarsheel: noble in behaviour.

Bhadrakapil: lord Shiva.

Bhadrashree: sandalwood tree.

Bhadravind: achieving good.

Bhadrāyu: leads a good life.

Bhadresh: lord of nobles, Shiva.

Bhadrik: noble.

Bhagāditya: wealth-bestowing sun.

Bhagan: next, of happy nature, joyful.

Bhagat: devotee.

Bhagavan: with great fortune, God, lord.

Bhagavant: with fortune, fortunate, shareholder.

Bhāgavat: spiritual being, Vishnu's follower, adorable, divine, glorious, happy, holy, illustrious, wealthy, Vishnu, Shiva, Krishna.

Bhagesh: lord of richness.

Bhagirath: one who brought Ganga on Earth.

Bhāgyanand: controller of destiny.

Bhāgyodhay: dawn of good luck.

Bhairav: fear-dispeller, frightening, formidable.

Bhajaman: praying deeply, praying fervently, praying sincerely.

Bhajan: devotional song, venerated, sacred.

Bhākosh: treasure of light, sun.

Bhakta: devotee, loyal, worshipper, honouring.

Bhaktarāj: king of devotees, best devotee.

Bhamhaghosh: chanting or recitation of Vedas.

Bhamhanand: happiness for knowledge.

Bhandil: fortune.

Bhānu: appearance, light, fame, glory, king, lord, master, Shiva, sun.

Bhānuchandra: shining moon.

Bhanudas: devotee of the sun.

Bhānudatta: sun-given, bright, sacred, illuminating.

Bhānudev: lord of glory, lord, sun.

Bhānuj: son of the sun.

Bhānukeshar: with rays as hair, sun.

Bhānumān: as bright as the sun.

Bhānumat: luminous, beautiful, enlightening, glorious, famous.

Bhanumitra: friend of sun/Planet Mercury.

Bhānunāth: lord of brightness.

Bhanuprakash: sun light.

Bhanuprasad: gift of sun.

Bharadwaj: a lucky bird, planet Mars.

Bharand: fulfiller, master, lord.

Bharaṇyu: attempting to fulfil, fire, friend, master, protector, moon, sun.

Bharat: fulfiller of all desires, well-maintained.

Bharat: India, universal monarch.

Bharav: bowstring.

Bhārgav: attaining radiance, archer, preceptor.

Bhārgavak: radiant, diamond.

Bharu: carrying the load, lord, master, gold, sea.

Bhārūp: with a splendid form, brilliant, shining, resplendent.

Bhāravi: protected by God, shining sun.

Bhāsant: illuminating, beautiful, radiant, shining splendid, sun, moon.

Bhāsin: shining, radiant, brilliant.

Bhāskar: sun, radiator, emitter of light, illuminator, gold, fire, hero, Shiva.

Bhāskari: son of the sun, bringer of glory.

Bhāsu: born of light, creator of light, sun.

Bhāsur: shining God, crystal, bright, divine, enlightening, glorious, hero, illuminating, sacred, splendid, venerated.

Bhāsvān: full of brightness.

Bhāsvar: luminious, enlightening, brilliant, resplendent, shining.

Bhaṭṭi: noble, meritorious, virtuous.

Bhātu: light, sun.

Bhaumendra: lord of the earth.

Bhaumik: being on earth.

Bhaumiratna: jewel of the earth, coral.

Bhautik: physical, corporeal, elemental, shining pearl, Shiva.

Bhauvan: belonging to the world.

Bhava: existing, feeling, sentiment, Shiva.

Bhavad: giving life, cause of existence.

Bhavadatta: given by Shiva.

Bhavadev: lord of existence, Shiva.

Bhāvaj: born of the heart.

Bhāvan: creator, welfare-promoter, heart-pleasing, forest of rays, illuminating, imagining, Krishna.

Bhavānand: that which delights Shiva, pleasure of existence, bliss in existence.

Bhavamanya: creator of the universe, universally accepted.

Bhavasāgar: ocean of worldly existence.

Bhavashekhar: Shiva's crest, moon.

Bhavesh: lord of worldly existence, Shiva.

Bhavik: well-meaning, happy, pious, righteous.

Bhavil: good.

Bhavin: living being, human.

Bhavish: striving to exist, lord of existence, Shiva.

Bhavishnu: knowing the future, fairing well, thriving.

Bhāvuk: sentimental, sensitive, aesthetic, prosperous.

Bhavun: pleasing, attractive.

Bhavya: magnificent, beautiful, excellent, existing suitably, fit, handsome, pious, proper, true.

Bhawanidas: devotee of Godess Durga.

Bheemachandra: moon of strength.

Bheemanāth: lord of strength.

Bheemaveg: swift, active, quick.

Bheemrāj: king of the powerful.

Bhikshit: obtained as alms.

Bhim: fearful.

Bhimsen: Shiva, Vishnu.

Bhishaj: healer, physician, medicine, curer.

Bhisham: Shiva.

Bhoja: bountiful, generous, liberal.

Bhojadev: fulfiller of desires.

Bhojarāj: lord of the generous.

Bholānāth: lord of the innocent, Shiva.

Bhonesh: lord of the universe.

Bhoumik: land owner.

Bhrāj: glittering, enlightening, illuminating, sacred, shining.

Bhrājat: shining, gleaming, glittering, shining, enlightening.

Bhudev: lord of earth.

Bhūdhan: one whose property is earth, king.

Bhūdhar: supporter of earth, mountain.

Bhuji: granting, favours, protector, patron.

Bhūman: consisting of all existing things, consisting of existence, earth.

Bhūmanyu: universally accepted, devotee of the earth.

Bhumat: possessing the earth, king.

Bhūmij: born of the earth.

Bhumindra: lord of the earth, king.

Bhuminjay: conqueror of the earth.

BhTūmya: belonging to the earth.

Bhūnandan: delighting the earth, son of earth, virtuous person.

Bhūpad: firm, stable.

Bhūpāl: guardian of the earth, king.

Bhūpat: lord of the earth.

Bhūpati: lord of the earth, Shiva.

Bhūpen: lord of the earth, king.

Bhūpendra: king of kings.

Bhupesh: king.

Bhūranya: worshipped by the world, active, eager, quick, Vishnu, sun.

Bhūri: abundant, divine, great, important, infinite, mighty, boundless.

Bhurid: donator in abundance.

Bhūridyumna: possessing great glory.

Bhūrikirti: very famous, very learned.

Bhūritejas: very glorious.

Bhūrivasu: very wealthy.

Bhūshakra: very renowned, powerful, venerated.

Bhūshan: ornament, embellishment, adornment, decoration.

Bhūtabhāvan: causing welfare of living beings, Vishnu, Shiva, Brahma.

Bhūtadhāman: dweller in substance, all-pervading, omnipresent.

Bhūtādi: originator of all beings, Supreme Spirit.

Bhūtajyoti: light of living beings.

Bhūtesh: lord of living beings, Brahma, Vishnu, Shiva.

Bhūtinand; bestower of pleasure.

Bhūvadvat: bestowing prosperity.

Bhūvan: being, earth, abode, human, living, being..

Bhuvanādeesh: master of the earth.

Bhuvanadeep: light of the earth.

Bhuvanapati: lord of the earth.

Bhuvanrāj: king of the earth.

Bhuvanesh: lord of the earth.

Bhuvangu: possessing the earth, sun, moon, fire.

Bhuvapati: lord of the atmosphere.

Bhuvas: air, atmosphere, heaven.

Bidūl: spotted, with an attractive body.

Bidyut: enlightened, full of knowledge, lightning, electricity, illumined.

Biman: honoured, respected from the heart.

Bimbeshwar: lord of sun and moon, lord of images, preceptor.

Bimbisār: essence of the Absolute.

Bimbit: reflected.

Bindeshwar: lord of creation, Supreme Lord.

Bindumādhav: thinker of the Absolute, well-read, illumined, enlightened, wise.

Bindumat: knower of truth, well-read, wise, wealthy enlightened, salvation-attainer.

Bindusār: an excellent pearl, essence of truth.

Bindusāras: concentrated, ocean of alphabets, well-read, wise, enlightened, venerated.

Binot: happy.

Binoy: humbleness, humility, request.

Bipin: forest, free, shelter-provider, magnificent.

Bipul: plenty, manifold, strong, much, many.

Biren: lord of warriors.

Birendra: lord of warriors.

Bireshwar: lord of warriors.

Birju: powerful.

Biswajit: victorious in the world.

Blake: fair-haired.

Bodh: knowledge, awakening, intelligence, thought, enlightenment, understanding.

Bonḍ: tiller of the soil.

Booker: beech tree.

Booth: hut.

Boyḍ: blonde, yellow.

Brahmadatta: given by Brahma, perfect, sacred.

Brahmadev: the Absolute, Brahma, God.

Brahmādya: beginning with Brahma, absolute, beginning.

Brahmagandh: fragrance of Brahma, fragrance of sacred knowledge.

Brahmagosh: sacred word, sacred syllable Om.

Brahmagiri: mountain of Brahma.

Brahmagupta: protected by Brahma.

Brahmajeet: winner of Brahma, self-controller, perfect, enlightened.

Brahmakrit: offering prayers, caused by Brahma, perfect, performed by the divine.

Brahmānand: bless, joy in Brahma, illumined, spiritually, enlightened, absolute pleasure.

Brahmāyush: existing as long as Brahma.

Branḍon: sword, fiery hill.

Brazil: brave, strong in conflict.

Brenṭ: steep hill.

Brian: strong.

Brihadātma: with a great soul, illumined, wise, enlightened.

Brihadguru: great master.

Brihant: massive, grand.

Brihaspati: lord of prayer, lord of devotion, lord of the powerful.

Brihat: abundant, lofty, tall, clear, large, loud, mighty, strong.

Brihatkirti: with infinite fame, renowned.

Brihit: nourished, cherished, strengthened.

Brijbhūshan: ornament of nature, Krishna.

Brijesh: lord of nature, Krishna.

Brijkishor: lord Krishna.

Brijmohan: universally attractive.

Brijnandan: lord Krishna.

Buḍ: herald, puff up, friend.

Buddhadatta: derived from enlightenment.

Buddhadev: lord of the wise, enlightened.

Buddhaghosh; voice of knowledge, speech of the enlightened.

Buddhagupta: protected by wisdom.

Buddhaguru: preceptor of the wise.

Buddhapāl: defender of the wise.

Buddhapriya: one liked by Buddha.

Buddharāj: lord of the wise.

Buddhirāj: lord of the intellect.

Budhan: awakening, wisdom, knowledge, sage, spiritual guide.

Budhil: wise, learned.

Budrik: learned, enlightened.

Bukka: heart, sentimental, loving, sincere.

Burhan: proof.

Burṭon: bright, fame.

C

Caḍman: warrior.

Calḍer: stream.

Calverṭ: shepherd.

Camlin: crooked line.

Carringṭon: beautiful.

Carṭer: cart driver.

Chaḍwick: warrior.

Chakeelā: charming, beautiful, brilliant, splendid, picturesque. .

Chāga: moisture, born of moisture.

Chhaila: handsome youth.

Chaitanya: consciousness, soul, spirit, mind, intelligence.

Chaitra: absorbed in pleasure, as pleasant as spring.

Chaitya: relevant to mind, individual soul.

Chaityak: abode of consciousness.

Chaka: contented, shining.

Chakor: shining, contented.

Chakradhar: one who carries Chakra (Krishna, Vishnu).

Chakradrish: round-eyed.

Chakrak: circular, wheel-like.

Chakrapani: lord Vishnu.

Chakravartin: powerful, renowned.

Chakshan̄: soothing, to the eyes, aspect, appearance.

Chakshas: look, appearance, radiance, teacher.

Chakshu: eye, sun god.

Chālak: driver, director, Supreme Soul.

Chalapati: lord of the moving, Vishnu.

Chaman: garden.

Chamarāj: leader of army.

Ċhāmikar: gold.

Champa: soother.

Champak: Champa (flower), Pagoda (flower).

Chanchu: famous, renowned, bird's beak.

Chandak: shining one, moon, moonlight, pleasing.

Chandakā: assuming any shape at will.

Chandan: sandalwood, auspicious, soothing.

Chandan: sandalwood, fragrant, auspicious, cool, soothing.

Chandanin: smeared with sandalwood paste, Shiva.

Chandānshee: hot-rayed, sun.

Chandas: moon-like.

Chandodev: lord of hymns, deity-invoker with hymns.

Chandra: bright shining, glittering, fair, radiant, moon, gold, silver, fair, water, red pearl.

Chandrabal: power of the moon.

Chandrabh: luminious like the moon.

Chandrabhān: as lustrous as the moon.

Chandrabhānu: radiant moon, venerated, illumined, renowned.

Chandrabhāsh: as brilliant as the moon, sword.

Chandrabhushan: lord Shiva.

Chandrabhūti: moon-born, silver.

Chandrachārya: moon among teachers, wise.

Chandradatta: moon-given, fair, tranquil, cool, soothing.

Chandradeep: moonlight.

Chandradhar: one who wears moon i.e. Lord Shiva.

Chandragupta: protected by moon.

Chandrahās: smile of the moon, daughter of the moon, moonlight, pleasing smile, glittering sword.

Chandraj: moon-born.

Chandrajit: conqueror of moon, excelling the moon.

Chandrajyot: moonlight.

Chandrak: crescent moon, moon.

Chandrak: peacock feather, moon.

Chandrakānt: as lovely as the moon, loved by the moon.

Chandrakesh: fair-haired.

Chandrakirañ: moonbeam.

Chandrakirti: as famous as the moon.

Chandrakriti: moon-shaped.

Chandralochan: moon-eyed.

Chandramādhav: honey of the moon, moonbeam.

Chandramauli: moon-crested, Shiva.

Chandramohan: as attractive as the moon.

Chandramukut: moon-crested, Shiva.

Chandrānan: moon-faced.

Chandranāth: lord of the moon, Shiva.

Chandranibhā: moonlike, bright, handsome.

Chandrānshu: moonbeam, with moon's lustre.

Chandrapād: feet of the moon, moonbeam.

Chandraprakāsh: moonlight.

Chandrashekhar: wearer of moon as crest jewel, Shiva.

Chandrashman: moonstone, cool, tranquil, soothing.

Chandrat: nectar of the moon, fair, handsome, nectar-like, tranquil.

Chandravimal: as pure as the moon.

Chandresh: lord of the moon, Shiva.

Chandril: moon-possessor, Shiva.

Chandrin: golden.

Chandroday: moonwise, inspiring love.

Chanduree: belonging to the moon, like the moon.

Chani: ruby.

Channa: renowned, famous.

Chapinan: merchant.

Chārañ: praise chanter.

Charañ: foot, support, good conduct, pillar.

Charañdās: devotee of the feet, respectful, worshipper.

Charanjit: one who has won over the Lord (Charanjeet).

Chāriman: beauty, movable.

Chārles: manly, strong.

Charmavān: protected, sheltered.

Chāru: agreeable, charming, beloved, beautiful, esteemed, saffron.

Chārudatta; born of beauty, extremely handsome.

Chāruhāsan: with a beautiful smile.

Chāruksar: of golden beauty.

Chārumat: intelligent.

Chārumod: pleasing, joy, gladness, jasmine.

Chārusār: essence of all that is beautiful, gold.

Chāruvardhan: enhancer of beauty.

Chāruvinda: attaining charm.

Chārvāk: sweet-tongued.

Chattradhār: bearer of the royal umbrella.

Chattravati: possessor of the umbrella of power.

Chaturanan: one with four heads i.e. Lord Bramha.

Chaturvedi: one who knows all the four Vedas.

Chavillākar: of handsome appearance.

Chāyan: moon.

Chāyānk: moon-like.

Chedi: intelligent, pleasant.

Chekitān: intelligent.

Chetak: thoughtful, jasmine.

Chetan: conscious, soul, animated, conspicious, distinguished, elegant, man, mind, visible.

Chetanya: cautious, intelligent, attentive.

Chetas: intelligence, consciousness, splendour, soul, mind, heart.

Chhailbehari: lord Krishna.

Chidakāsh: universal soul, Absolute Brahma.

Chidambar: with heart as vast as the sky.

Chidānand: ultimate bliss.

Chidātma: pure intelligence.

Chidātmat: consisting of pure thought.

Chidghan: full of knowledge.

Chidullās: with radiant thoughts, wise, spirtually enlightened.

Chihir: a bird.

Chikit: experienced, well read, enlightened, wise.

Chikka: small mouse.

Chikur: mountain, hair on the head.

Chiman: curious.

Chinmaya: consisting of pure intelligence, Supreme Spirit.

Chintāmaṇi: gem of thought, gem that fulfils desires, Brahma.

Chintāmukta: free from worry.

Chintan: thought, intellect, mind, meditation, perception.

Chintya: worthy of thought, worthy of being conceived.

Chirag: lamp.

Chirājush: favoured with long life.

Chiranjeet, Chirayu: immortal.

Chiranjeev: long lived. immortal.

Chiranjeevan: long-lived, infinite.

Chirantak: eternal.

Chiravāsas: long-lived.

Chitadhan: the conscious, Brahma.

Chiṭak: neck ornament, necklace.

Chitapati: lord of intellect, lord of thought.

Chitāyu: thought-descendant, intellect-born.

Chitrabāṇ: owner of variegated arrows.

Chitrabhānu: of variegated lustre, beautiful sun, multicoloured, lit, shining, sun, Shiva.

Chitrabhūta: painted, decorated.

Chitradarshi: seeing clearly, with bright observation.

Chitradharman: follower of various strange customs,

arrangement of various colours.

Chitragupta: secret picture, protected by the wonderful.

Chitragupta: lord Yama's helper who is records all deeds.

Chitrak: painted, spotted, beautiful, brave, bright, powerful, leopard, tiger.

Chitrakarman: doer of odd acts.

Chitraketu: possessor of a picturesque banner, Krishna.

Chitrāksha: speckle-eyed, with beautiful eyes, with mystic eyes.

Chitranāth: excellent lord.

Chitranga: with multi-hued body, antelope, vermilion.

Chitrapaksh: with dotted wings.

Chitrarashnu: with variegated rays, hibiscus.

Chitravāj: having wonderful riches.

Chitravansu: with many treasures, rich in shining stars.

Chitresh: wonderful lord.

Chitrūp: in the form of consciousness, wise, intelligent, good-hearted.

Chitta: intellect, mind, reason, thought.

Chitta: knowledge, consciousness, Brahma.

Chittabhog: fully conscious, mind-enjoyer, wise, intelligent, thoughtful.

Chittahārin: capturer of heart.

Chittaj: born of the heart.

Chittanāth: lord of the soul, Supreme Being.

Chittapar: beyond reason, Supreme Being.

Chittaprabha: light of the soul.

Chittaprasad: happiness.

Chittaprasād: gift of mind, mind-pleasing, charming.

Chittaprasanna: mentally happy, cheerful, making others happy.

Chittaranjan: pleasing the mind, charming, loving.

Chittaswarup: the supreme spirit.

Chittavat: with a heart, understanding, kind-hearted.

Chittayu: son of the heart, mind-born.

Chittesh: ruler of mind.

Chittin: thinker, wise, intelligent.

Chitvan: glance, a look.

Chitvat: blessed with wisdom, reasonable, logical.

Choksha: pure, agreeable, clean, pleasant.

Chudamani: the best, crest Jewel.

Chunchu: renowned.

Chyavan: moving, agile, active.

Chitraashva: varigated horse.

Chilāka: necklace.

Chikura: a lock of hair.

Chhattra Nilaya: college

Chetās: intelligent.

Chaka: to shine.

Clārk: scholar, cleric.

Clayṭon: clay, clay farm.

Cliffoṛḍ: land near hill.

Clive: cliff dweller.

Clinṭon: town near a hill.

Coḍy: assistant, cushion, possession.

Colin: youth, child, victor.

Coman: noble.

Conan: wise.

Conner: desire, wish.

Courṭney: from the court.

Cullen: handsome, young animal.

Cahavāka: honey tongued.

Chetonārē: attractive.

Chhāgali: name of the prince.

Chag: love.

Chaidya: administrator.

Chitārathi: having beautiful chariot.

D

Daha: blazing, very bright.

Dahan: burning, destroying.

Daityāri: enemy of demons.

Daivya: divine, glorious.

Dakeshaketu: with a golden banner.

Daksha: able, energetic, fire, gold, perfect, talented.

Dakshesh: lord Shiva.

Dakshānil: perfect breeze.

Dakshapati: lord of the perfect.

Dākshi: golden son, son of a perfect being.

Dakshin̄: right, able, candid, clever, fit, south, sincere, sense of direction.

Dalakamal: lotus.

Dalamodak: petal honey.

Dama: wealth, home, house, self-restraint.

Dāman: rope, girdle, wreath.

Daman: training, subduing, suppressing, self-controlled, overpowering.

Damanak: subduer, brave, conqueror, power, victor.

Damati: conqueror, subduer.

Damayitri: tamer, subduer, Vishnu, Shiva.

Dambar: self-restrained.

Dambha: pride, ego.

Damik: land, earth, field.

Damin: self-controlled.

Dāmodar: Krishna.

Damosh: wealthy, bound, fortunate.

Danah: intelligent, full of knowledge.

Danya: tameable.

Dānapati: lord of benevolence, lord of generosity.

Dānasāgar: ocean of generosity.

Dānav: valiant, conqueror, victor.

Dānaveer: hero among donors, extremely generous.

Dānavendra: lord of the brave.

Danḍashree: best among the staff, best judge, best manager.

Danḍarvat: carrying a staff, leader, commander, full of self-respect.

Dānu: courageous, contentment, liberal, prosperity, air, wind.

Danijadveesh: enemy of demons.

Darādish: king.

Dārak: breaking, splitting.

Darpa: pride, arrogance.

Darpan: mirror.

Darphan: destroyer of ego, Shiva.

Darphar: ego-destroyer Shiva.

Darpak: pride.

Darpaṅ: creating vanity, mirror.

Ḍarrel: beloved.

Darsha: worth looking at, Krishna.

Darshan: seeing, audience, discernment, vision, philosophy, showing.

Darshanpāl: protector of sight, scholar of philosophy.

Darshish: powerful, mighty.

Daruka: deodar tree.

Daruṅ: as hard as wood.

Dārvanda: peacock.

Darveek: wind.

Darvi: wooden ladle.

Ḍārwin: beloved.

Dashadyu: very powerful.

Dashajyoti: whose glory spreads in 10 directions.

Dasharāj: master of the 10 directions, master of the universe.

Dashrat: making things visible, beautiful, conspicuous, glowing, visible, moon, sun.

Dasharath: one with ten chariots, Lord Raṃ's father.

Dasmat: desirable acceptable.

Dasmay: beautiful.

Dasra: doing wonderful deeds, aiding.

Dāshu: worshipping, sacrificing.

Dāshūr: holy, pious.

Datta: given, granted, presented.

Dattātman: given the soul, with total mind concentration, conducting duty sincerely, businessman.

Dattatreya: three-headed divinity of Vishnu-Shiva-Brahma.

Dattey: lord Indra.

Dattoli: fully engrossed.

Dattravat: rich in gifts.

Daulat: wealth, riches.

Daya: mercy.

Dāyād: son, inheritor.

Dayākar: compassionate, Shiva.

Dayākūrcha: mine of compassion.

Dayāl: compassionate, merciful, tender.

Dayān: honest, truthful.

Dayanand: one who likes being merciful or kind.

Dayaneet: compassionate conduct.

Dayānidhi: treasurer house of mercy.

Dayārām: full of mercy.

Dayāsāgar: ocean of compassion.

Dayaswarup: merciful.

Day āveer: heroically compassionate.

Dayit: worthy of compassion, beloved, cherished, dear.

Ḍayṭon: bright.

Deedhitimat: shining, brilliant, sun.

Deekshin: initiated, consecrated.

Deekshit: initiated, consecrated.

Deenabandhu: friend of the poor, Supreme Spirit.

Deendayāl: being kind to the poor.

Deep: illuminator, enlightener, lamp, light, lantern.

Deepak: lamp, inflaming, illuminating, kindling, saffron.

Deepānkar: causer of light.

Deepākur: lamp flame.

Deepen: lord of the lamp, light of the lamp.

Deependra: lord of light.

Deependu: moon.

Deepesh: lord of light, sun.

Deepin: inflaming, illuminated, excited, manifested.

Deepta: illuminated, blazing, brilliant, gleaming, hot, shining.

Deeptāgni: blazing fire.

Deeptaketu: bright-bannered.

Deeptakirti: very famous.

Deeptānshu: bright-rayed, sun.

Deeptendu: shining moon.

Deepti: light, beauty, splendour.

Deeptimān: bright, shining, radiant.

Deeptopal: brilliant gem, white, topaz.

Deergha: lofty, deep high, tall, Shiva.

Dehaja: born of body, child.

Deheshwar: lord of the body, corporeal, earth.

Ḍenver: green valley.

Ḍermotṭ: free of envy.

Ḍerry: great lover.

Deshak: director, guide, ruler, preceptor.

Ḍesmond: man of the world.

Deva: light, a God, divine, deity.

Devachandra: moon among Gods.

Devachitta: will of the Gods.

Devadarsh: preceptor of the divine, observer of the Gods.

Devadatta: God-given.

Devadeep: lamp of the Gods, eye.

Devaguru: preceptor of the Gods, father of the Gods.

Devahas: divine duck, divine swan.

Devahū: invoking the Gods.

Devaj: born of the Gods.

Devajūt: attached to the Gods, inspired by the Gods.

Devak: heavenly, Godly, celestial.

Devakām: pious, striving for divinity, loving the Gods.

Devakānt: beloved of the Gods.

Devakirti: with heavenly fame.

Devakumār: son of a God.

Devamadan: gladdening the Gods, inspiring the Gods.

Devamadhu: divine nectar.

Devamāṇak: jewel of the Gods.

Devamanjar: divine jewel.

Devamay: consisting of the Gods, abode of all virtues.

Devanaman: bowing to the Gods.

Devānand: joy of the Gods.

Devanandin: amusing the Gods.

Devanāth: lord of the Gods, Shiva.

Devanāyak: leader of the Gods.

Devang: part of God.

Devānsh: partial incarnation of the Gods.

Devanūchar: follower of the Gods.

Devapālit: protected by the Gods.

Devāpi: friend of the Gods.

Devaprasād: given by the Gods.

Devapūjit: worshipped by the Gods, Krishna.

Devapushpa: flower of the Gods.

Devarāj: king of the Gods.

Devarām: absorbed in divine deeds, meritorious, venerated, virtuous.

Devārāṇya: garden of the Gods.

Devarāt: delighting in the Gods, pious, God-given, religious.

Devārpaṇ: offering to the Gods.

Devarsi: sage of Devas.

Devarshi: a sage among Gods.

Devarya: divine belief.

Devasheesh: blessing of the Gods.

Devashikhar: divine diadem.

Devashinsu: divine child.

Devasmit: with a divine smile.

Devashrū: known to the Gods.

Devashrut: with divine knowledge.

Devashūr: divine hero.

Devatajit: conquering the Gods.

Devatāras: freed by the Gods, God-like.

Devātman: divine soul.

Devavarsh: divine year.

Devavee: pleasing the Gods, devotee, worshipper, priest.

Devayān: leading to the Gods, vehicle of God.

Devayashas: divine glory.

Devdas: servant of Lord, a servant of temple.

Deveesh: chief of the Gods, Brahma, Vishnu, Shiva.

Devejya: preceptor of the Gods.

Devendra: chief of the Gods.

Devesh: God Indra.

Deveshit: sent by the Gods.

Deveshṭha: best among the Gods.

Deveshu: divine arrow.

Deveshwar: lord of the Gods.

Devevarya: best of the Gods.

Devidās: slave of the Goddess.

Devila: pious, attached to the Gods, venerated, righteous.

Devilal: son of Godess.

Devin: resembling a God.

Deviprasād: gift of the Goddess.

Devkinandan: son of Devki - (Lord Krishna).

Devon: defender.

Devtadeep: king of Gods.

Devya: divine power.

Dhāma: ray, house, light, majesty, place of pilgrimage, splendour, strength.

Dhāmādip: lord of rays.

Dhāman: ray, abode, glory, house, light, majesty, splendour, strength.

Dhāmahidhi: treasure of splendour.

Dhāmavat: house owner, strong, powerful.

Dhanad: wealth, bestowing.

Dhanadeshwar: wealth-giving lord.

Dhanādhip: lord of wealth.

Dhanajit: wealth, winner of wealth.

Dhananad: pleasure of having wealth.

Dhananjay: fire, conqueror of wealth, victorious.

Dhanapāl: guardian of wealth, king.

Dhanapati: lord of wealth.

Dhanavant: possessing wealth.

Dhanavardhan: increasing wealth.

Dhanavant: containing wealth, sea.

Dhanāyush: with a rich life.

Dhanesh: lord of wealth.

Dhaneshwar: lord of wealth.

Dhanin: wealthy.

Dhanaraj: king of wealth (Kuber).

Dhanva: with a bow.

Dhanvantari: doctor of Gods.

Dhanvin: armed with a bow.

Dhāraṅ: bearing, holding, keeping, resembling.

Dharam: virtue, duty, justice, faith, honesty.

Dharaṅidhar: supporting the earth, tortoise, king, Vishnu, Krishna.

Dharaṅija: born of the earth.

Dharāpati: lord of the earth, Vishnu.

Dharendra: king of the earth.

Dharesh: king, Lord of land.

Dharma: path of life, duty, justice, law, established, observance, practice, religion, righteousness.

Dharmadev: lord of law.

Dharmayū: one who lives for righteousness.

Dharmendra: lord of righteousness.

Dharmesh: lord of righteousness.

Dharuṇ: bearing, holding, supporting, Brahma.

Dhātā: establisher, founder, supporter, creator, Brahma.

Dhātri: establisher, creator, supporter, founder.

Dhaumya: grey, smoky.

Dhāvak: turner, swift, quick, flowing.

Dhaval: fair complexioned.

Dhavala: dazzling white, beautiful, handsome.

Dhavesh: God.

Dhavit: whitish, purified, clean, washed.

Dheemān: possessed with wisdom.

Dheemant: possessed with wisdom, learned, intelligent.

Dheemat: wise, intelligent, sensible, learned.

Dheera: patient, intelligent, skilful, tolerant, wise.

Dheeradhi: mine of tolerance.

Dheeraj: full of tolerance, creator of tolerance, born of patience.

Dheerchetas: patient mind, strong-minded, courageous.

Dheeresh: lord of tolerance.

Dheetik: thoughtful, wise.

Dhiraṇ: wise.

Dhiren: one who is strong, powerful.

Dhirendra: patience.

Dhrishaj: bold, hero.

Dhrishamān: bold, confident.

Dhrishit: bold, brave, daring.

Dhrishni: ray of light.

Dhrishṭa: audacious, bold, brave, confident.

Dhrisṭak: bold, brave, audacious.

Dhrita: held, borne, pledged, fixed, upon, maintained.

Dhritak: bearer of constancy.

Dhritārchis: of constant splendour, Vishnu.

Dhritātman: steady mind, calm, firm.

Dhriti: patience, resolution, virtue.

Dhruv: constant, eternal, firm, fixed, permanent, polar, star, Brahma, Vishnu, Shiva.

Dhruvak: firm, stable post, stake.

Dhruvi: firmly fixed.

Dhūmaketu: smoke-bannered, fire, comet, sun.

Dhūpāl: fragrant.

Dhyān: meditation.

Dhyanesh: lord of meditation.

Degeesh: lord of direction.

Digamber: nacked, Lord Shiva.

Digjay: conqueror of all directions, sky-clad.

Digvijay: conqueror of all directions.

Dikpāl: protector of a direction.

Dikshit: initiated into a religious order.

Dileep: giver-acceptor, generous king.

Diler: proud, courageous.

Diljeet: winner of heart.

Dilvar: beloved.

Dinādeesh: God of the day, sun.

Dinajyotish: illuminating the day, sunshine.

Dinakānth: sun.

Dinakar: that which causes day, sun.

Dinakshay: decline of day, evening.

Dinanath: saviour of the downtrodden or poor.

Dinant: end of day, evening, dusk.

Dinapāl: sun.

Dinarāj: sun.

Dinesh: lord of the day, sun.

Dineshwar: lord of the day, sun.

Dishāpāl: guardian of a direction.

Dishṭa: settled, assigned, directed, appointed, fixed.

Ditakiraṅ: hot-rayed, sun.

Ditikar: bringing glow, radiating, illuminating.

Ditimat: glowing, brilliant, bright, radiant, splendid.

Divākar: day-maker, sun.

Divi: the blue jay bird.

Divij: sky-born, heaven-born, celestial, God.

Divijāt: sky-born, heaven-born.

Divikshay: dwelling in heaven.

Divirath: sky-chariot, sun.

Diviyaj: praying to heaven.

Diviyoni: sky-born.

Divoj: descended from heaven.

Divyānshu: divine light, sun.

Divyendu: moonlight.

Divyesh: sun.

Ḍonalḍ: ruler of the world.

Ḍonnelly: brave black man.

Doshakar: night-maker, moon.

Ḍrake: ale, duck, dragon.

Dravid: property-owner, landlord, wealthy.

Dravin̄: movable property.

Drishāhi: full of light, sun.

Drisheek: good-looking, splendid.

Druha: son.

Drupad: firm-footed, pillar, column.

Dūlāl: lovable youth.

Dulee: happy.

Ḍuncan: dark-skinned warrior.

Durādhar: invincible, irresistible.

Duranjaya: a heroic son.

Durāp: inaccessible.

Durgadas: servant (a devotee) of Godess Durga.

Durgadās: given by Durga.

Durgadatta: given by Durga.

Durgam: difficult to travel over, unattainable, impassable.

Durgesh: lord of fort.

Duritākshay: sinless, with sins destroyed.

Durjay: difficult to conquer, invincible, irresistable, Vishnu.

Durlabh: extraordinary, unattainable, dear, eminent, rare.

Durvār: irresistible.

Durvartu: irresistible.

Durvesh: Shiva.

Durvish: one who cannot be affected by poison, Shiva.

Duryodhan: invincible.

Dushyant: destroyer of evil.

Ḍusṭin: valiant fighter, dark stone.

Dwarkadhish: ruler of Dwarka (Lord Krishna).

Dwarkanath: lord of Dwarka (Lord Krishna).

Dwarakesh: lord of Dwarka, Krishna.

Ḍwighṭ: fair.

Dwijendra: moon.

Dwijesh: moon.

Dyota: light, brilliance.

Dyuchar: walking through the heavens.

Diyujaya: victory over the heaven.

Diyuksha: celestial.

Dyumana: glorious, energy.

Dyumni: powerful, splendid.

Dyuneesh: day and night.

Dyumat: bright, brilliant, excellent, splendid, strong.

Dyumna: splendour, glory, inspiration, majesty, power.

Dyuneesh: day and night, night-like virtues.

Dyupati: sky-lord, sun.

Dyutan: shining, radiant, bright.

Dyuti: brightness, lustre, majesty, splendour, radiance.

Dyutikar: brightness, lustre, majesty, splendour, radiance.

Dyutimān: heavenly, bright, majestic resplendent.

Dyutit: bright, clear, illuminated, shining.

Dyutȧna: bright.

Dwipāda: two legged.

Dwija: born twice.

Dulee: joyous.

Druha: son.

E

Edan: flame.

Eḍdie: defender of property.

Edha: type of wood, holy, sacred.

Edhas: sacred wood, happiness.

Edhati: born of wood, fire, man, happiness, prosperity.

Edhit: grown, evolved, increased, progressed.

Eḍmonḍ: prosperous.

Eḍwarḍ: guardian of property.

Eḍwin: gainer of property.

Egan: ardent.

Eha: desired, Vishnu.

Ehsān: obligation, gratefulness.

Ekachit: with one mind, with concentration, poise.

Ekadā: the first one, giver of one, the Absolute.

Ekadyū: supreme sky.

Ekāgra: concentrated, attentive, calm, stable, tranquil.

Ekahams: the only swan, soul.

Ekak: one, sole.

Ekāksha: single-eyed, one with an excellent eye.

Ekākshar: imperishable, letter Om, single syllable.

Ekalā: solitary.

Ekalinga: lord Shiva.

Ekam: one, peerless, unique, the Absolute.

Ekāmbar: with sky as attire.

Ekanai: only leader.

Ekanāth: only master.

Ekanāyak: sole leader, Shiva.

Ekānga; single-bodied, rare, only one, unique, Vishnu.

Ekānsh: single part, whole, one.

Ekāntin: devoted to single object.

Ekarāj: sole monarch.

Ekarāya: sole ruler.

Ekasarga: closely attentive, concentrated.

Ekātan: closely attentive, concentrated.

Ekātma: one universal soul.

Ekayān: worldly wisdom, following the doctrine of unity.

Ekayāvan: wise one.

Ekindra: sole lord, Supreme Being.

Ekesh: sole God, Supreme Being.

Ekeshwar: sole God, Supreme Being.

Ekish: one God, primal God.

Ekta: unity, union.

Eashāna: name of the heaven.

Edhitā: increased.

Edi: healing.

Elash: shining.

Eleazer: God has helped.

Elesh: king.

Elṭon: from the old estate.

Emir: charming prince.

Emūsh: lifter.

Eṅa: doe, spotted, black antelope.

Erin: peace.

Esh: god.

Eshaṅ: desire, aim, wish, Shiva.

Eshika: target-reacher, arrow, dart.

Eshitā: desired.

Eshwar: god.

Eshwardutt: gift of God.

Esmonḍ: protective, grace.

Evān: young warrior.

Ezrā: help.

Eil: son of the earth.

Eka: only one.

Eta: painted.

F

Fābā: bean.

Faber: craftsman.

Fabian: cautiously persistent, bean.

Fadi: redeemer.

Faghyār: intelligent, scholar.

Faham: wise, considerate.

Fahd: lynx.

Fahim: learned, wise, prudent.

Faisal: decisive.

Faishāh: principal, chief.

Faizāh: attaining, accomplishing.

Faizān: charitable, beneficent.

Fakāh: gay, happy.

Fākhir: proud, excellent.

Fakhr: pride, fame, jewellery, excellence, nobility.

Fakht: moonlight.

Fālgun: month of a Hindu calendar.

Falih: prosperous.

Faliq: creator.

Faloday: pleasure, happiness.

Faqid: intelligent, wise.

Faraj: ease, relief, joy.

Fareed: unique, pearl, God, exquisite.

Farhān: joy, happiness.

Farhāt: happiness, joy.

Fāris: horseman.

Farjat: happiness.

Farmān: command, order, royal patent.

Farmand: intelligent, pure.

Farooq: he who distinguishes from falsehood.

Fartash: existence.

Farūd: solitary, unique.

Farūh: gaiety, joy.

Farūz: turquoise.

Faryād: complaint, surprise, entreaty for help.

Farzand: son, child.

Fās: firm, council.

Fātih: Prophet Muhammed's name.

Fātir: originator.

Fatiq: east, bright, dawn, shining.

Fausṭ: fortunate.

Favian: brave.

Fawāz: successful.

Fayyāz: generous, charitable, bountiful, merciful.

Fazil: talented, scholar.

Felipe: lover of horses.

Ferḍinanḍ: ready traveller.

Fergus: of manly, strength.

Fernānḍo: ready traveller.

Ferris: rock, iron.

Finlay: fair, hero, sun beam.

Firōh: happiness, joy.

Faiyaz: artistic.

Faiz: profit.

Fanindra: Sheshnaaga.

Fatika: crystal

Firyāl: adornment.

Flemming: native of Flanders.

Fletcher: arrow maker.

Florence: flourishing, booming, prosperous.

Floyd: gray.

Flynn: son of a redhead.

Floyḍ: hollow.

Forbes: prosperous.

Forḍ: river crossing.

Francis: of France.

Frank: spear.

Frazier: strawberry.

Freḍerick: peaceful.

Fulochan: with merry eyes.

Fularvind: full-blown lotus flower.

Furozan: bright, shining, radiant.

Fannibhushan: Lord Shiva.

Fanniga: Lord Vishnu.

Fannisa: serpent.

Firdaus: victory.

G

Gabriel: archangel.

Gadhi: seeker of knowledge, one who stands.

Gagan: moving one, sky, heaven.

Gaganātmaj: descendant of heaven, divine nectar.

Gaganechar: moving through the air, birds, planets, celestials.

Gajarāj: lord of elephants.

Gajānan: Ganesha.

Gajāri: enemy of elephants, lion, Shiva.

Gajendra: lord of elephants.

Gajendranath: owner of Gajendra (Lord Indra).

Gajeshṭha: best among elephants.

Gajānan: lotus root.

Gālava: to worship.

Gamal: camel.

Gambheer: deep, considerate, grave, influential, patient, serious, thoughtful.

Gaṅadhyaksh: leader of the troops, Shiva.

Gaṅapati: lord of the troops.

Ganaraj: lord of the clan.

Gandhadhārin: possessing perfumes, Shiva.

Gandhamād: delighting with fragrance.

Gandhamādan: intoxicating with perfume, large black bee.

Gandhamālin: with fragrant garlands.

Gandhapālilṅ: protector of fragrance, Shiva.

Gandhār: fragrance.

Gandharāj: king of fragrance, Cape jasmine.

Gandhārin: fragrant, Shiva.

Gandharva: celestial musician, cuckoo, sun God.

Gàndhasoma: with perfumed juice, white water lily.

Gandesh: lord of fragrance.

Gāndeer: hero.

Gaṇḍeeva: illuminator of the earth, conquering the earth, magical bow that is beyond damage.

Ganendra: lord of a troop.

Ganesh: lord of troops, elephant-God.

Gangadās: devotee of Ganga.

Gangādhar: holding the Ganga, Shiva.

Gangadutt: gift of Ganga.

Gangāl: of the Ganga, beryl.

Ganganāth: lord of Ganga, Shiva.

Gangesh: lord Shiva.

Gangeya: of Ganga.

Gangodak: water of Ganga river.

Gaṅin: one with attendants.

Ganjan: surpassing, conquering, excelling.

Ganmanya: distinguished, notable, honoured, respected.

Garfield: promontory.

Garg: gull.

Gariman: heaviness.

Gartesh: master of cave.

Garula: carrier of the great.

Garutmat: winged, protector against poison.

Garvishth: extremely proud.

Gaṛy: spear carrier.

Gāthā: strong, song, verse.

Gāthin: storyteller, singer.

Gatālin: with a rhythmic gait.

Gātra: body, corporeal.

Gātravat: with a beautiful body.

Gātravind: having a body.

Gātū: singer, song, Indian cuckoo.

Gauchar: cow-like, white, cow-coloured, pearl.

Gaunārda: celebrated bringer of light, enlightening, illuminating.

Gaura: cow-coloured, fair, beautiful, Shiva, moon, beech tree.

Gaurang: fair complexioned, Vishnu, Shiva, Krishna.

Gaurav: glory, dignity, esteem, prestige, gravity.

Gaureesh: lord of Gauri, Shiva.

Gauresh: lord of Gauri, Shiva.

Gaurikānt: beloved of Gauri, Shiva.

Gaurinandan: son of Gauri (Lord Ganesh, Kartikeya).

Gaurināth: lord of Gauri, Shiva.

Gauriprasanna: pleaser of Gauri, Shiva.

Gaurish: lord Shiva.

Gaurishankar: lord Shiva and Gauri (Parvati).

Gautam: dispeller of darkness.

Gavāksh: bull's eye, window.

Gaveeshṭha: abode of light, emitter of light.

Gaveeshwar: lord of oxen.

Gavendra: lord of oxen, bull, Vishnu.

Gaveshin: seeking.

Gāyak: singer, wealthy, offspring.

Gayan: singing, vocal music.

Gayand: tusker.

Gayarājan: king of songs.

Geet: song.

Geoffrey: heavenly place.

Ghanapriya: lover of clouds (peacock).

Ghanarām: cloud, dependant, abode of clouds, garden.

Ghanashyām: as dark as cloud, Krishna.

Ghanendra: lord of clouds (Lord Indra).

Ghansar: fragrant, auspicious, sacred, camphor.

Ghanteshwar; lord of bells.

Ghantin: one who sounds like a bell, Shiva.

Gilroy: servant of the king.

Ginṭon: garden.

Givendra: Shivā.

Giri: mountain, cloud, ball.

Giribāndhav: friend of mountains, Shiva.

Giridhar: holder of mountain, Krishna.

Giridhāri: mountain-holder, Krishna.

Girijanandan: son of Girija (Lord Ganesh).

Girijānāth: lord of Parvati, Shiva.

Girijāpati: lord of Parvati, Shiva.

Girijaprasād: given with Parvati's blessings.

Girijavar: best among rocks.

Girika: heart of the Gods.

Girikshit: dwelling on the mountain, Shiva.

Girilāl: son of mountain lord.

Girimān: like a mountain, powerful elephant.

Girinandan: son of mountain lord.

Girināth: lord of the mountains, Shiva.

Girindra: lord of speech, Shiva, highest mountain.

Giripati: lord of the mountain, Shiva.

Girirāj: king of the mountains.

Girish: lord of speech, lord of mountain, Shiva.

Girivar: excellent mountain, Krishna.

Godil: harbour.

Godhārin: cow-keeper, cowherd, Krishna.

Godwin: friend of God.

Gogan: multitude of rays.

Goman: rich in herds.

Gomin: cattle owner.

Gonand: son of a cow.

Gondesh: Shiva.

Gopā: herdsman, guardian of cows.

Gopāl: protector of cows, cowherd, Krishna.

Gopālak: protector of cows.

Gopan: protection.

Gopānandan: son of a cowherd, Krishna.

Gopati: cow-owner, leader, sun, chief, Vishnu, Shiva, Krishna.

Gopendra: lord of cowherds, Krishna.

Gopesh: chief of herdsmen, Krishna.

Gopichandan: sandalpaste of the herdswomen.

Gopichandra: moon of the herdswomen, Krishna.

Gopikrishna: Krishna-Radha conjoined.

Gopināth: lord of herdswomen.

Gopit: hidden, preserved, guarded, wagtail.

Gorala: likeable.

Goshālak: master of cowherds.

Gosharya: dawn.

Gotam: best among the arise.

Govind: master of the mountain.

Govindadatta: given by Krishna.

Graharāj: lord of planets, sun.

Graharājan: king of planets, sun.

Graheesh; lord of the planets, sun.

Grahin: of planets, woodapple.

Grahìsh: lord of the planets, sun.

Granger: farmer.

Granthik: tier of knots, composer, astrologer, narrator.

Greg: fierce.

Gregory: vigilant.

Griheet: taken up, understood, accepted.

Gudakesh: Arjun of *Mahabharata*.

Guha: secret one.

Gulāb: rose.

Gulshan: garden.

Guṅadhār: bearer of attributes.

Guṅādhya: rich in virtues.

Guṅākar: mine of virtues.

Guṅamidhi: treasure of virtues.

Gunaratna: jewel of virtue.

Guṅasāgar: ocean of virtue, Brahma.

Guṅasharman: abode of qualities.

Guṅashekhar: virtue-crested.

Gunāvaraṅ: on the virtue path.

Guṇavat: virtuous.

Guṇayukta: endowed with virtue.

Gunesh: lord of virtues, mountain.

Guṇin: endowed with virtues.

Gunja: well-woven.

Gunjik: humming, meditation, reflection.

Guṇottam: with excellent qualities.

Guptak: protected.

Gurbachan: promise or words of the guru.

Gurdayal: compassionate guru.

Guru: preceptor, teacher, master, priest, spiritual, guide.

Gurucharan: at the guru's feet.

Gurudā: god-given, Vishnu.

Gurudar: intellectual.

Gurudās: guru's servant.

Gurudatta: given by the guru.

Gālava: name of the tree.

Godin: armed with club.

Gurudev: divine guru.

Gurudeep: lamp of the guru.

Gurumeet: friend of the guru.

Gurumee: one with the guru.

Gurunām: name of the guru.

Guruṇāth: lord of the gurus, Supreme Being.

Guruprasād: guru's blessings.

Gururāj: lord of the spiritual teachers.

Gurusharaṇ: in the guru's protection.

Gurusimran: in remembrance of the guru.

Guruttam: best teacher, Vishnu.

Guruveer: warrior of the guru.

Guruwant: virtuous.

Gutsak: cluster of blossoms.

Gwalip: proud.

Guālipa: pride.

Grridhu: Lord Kāma.

H

Habib: beloved.

Hadi: guiding to the light.

Hadiyā: guiding to righteousness.

Hafiz: protected.

Haifā: slender.

Hakesh: lord of sound.

Halik: ploughman.

Halikshan̄: fleet-footed animal, lion.

Halin: ploughman.

Hameed: friend.

Hamilṭon: beautiful mountain.

Hans: swan, duck, gander, goose, flamingo, ascetic, pure person, individual soul, Supreme Soul, Shiva, Vishnu.

Hansachūḍ: swan crest.

Hansrāj: son of a swan.

Hansakāy: group of swans.

Hansaraj: king of swans.

Hansarath: with swan as chariot, Brahma.

Hansārudh: mounted on swan, Brahma.

Hansin: containing the universal soul, Krishna.

Hansapāl: lord of the swan, Brahma.

Hanugiri: mountain of Hanuman.

Hanumān: heavy-jawed.

Hanumant: heavy-jawed.

Hanumesh: lord of Hanuman, Rama.

Haraswarūp: in the image of Shiva.

Hạratejas: Shiva's energy.

Haraveer: warrior of God.

Haren̄u: respectable.

Haresh: lord Shiva.

Hareshit: cheerful, gay.

Hari: yellow, green, tawny, parrot, cuckoo, peacock, man, ray of light, fire, wind, sun, moon, Brahma, Vishnu, Shiva.

Hariaksh: Vishnu's eye, lion's eye, the pivot of Vishnu, Shiva.

Haribhadra: auspicious, as beautiful as Vishnu.

Haribhajan: hymn to Vishnu.

Harichandan: sandalpaste of Hari, yellow moonlight saffron.

Harichāp: Indra's low, railnbow.

Haricharan: at Vishnu's feet.

Haridās: Vishnu's servant.

Haridatta: blessings of Vishnu, given by Vishnu.

Haridhām: abode of Vishnu.

Haridhan: Vishnu's wealth.

Haridra: yellow, turmeric.

Harihar: lord Vishu and Lord Shiva together.

Hārij: horizon.

Harikānt: dear to Indra, beautiful like a lion.

Harilāl: son of Vishnu.

Harin̄: yellowish white, deer, attractive, goose, gazelle, antelope, pearl-garlanded, sun, Vishnu, Shiva.

Harināksh: doe-eyed, Shiva.

Harin̄ānka: marked like a deer, camphor.

Harinesh: lord of the deer, lion.

Haripāl: defending Vishnu, lion.

Hariprasād: blessing of Vishnu.

Haripreet: beloved of Vishnu.

Harirāj: king of lions.

Harish: Vishnu-Shiva conjoined.

Harishankar: lord Vishnu and Lord Shankar (Shiva).

Harishar: with Vishnu as an arrow, Shiva.

Harishchandra: with golden splendour, full of patience, Vishnu-moon conjoined.

Harishipra: ruddy-cheeked.

Harishrāvā: praising Hari.

Harita: lion, sun, green, verdant, yellow, pale, red, tawny, turmeric, Vishnu.

Hārit: green, moderate wind.

Hārivās: with the fragrance of Hari.

Harivatsa: beloved of Vishnu.

Harley: army, meadow.

Harmendra: moon.

Harolḍ: army power.

Haroshit: very happy, joyful.

Harsha: joy, delilght.

Harshad: very happy.

Harshak: delighting, gladdening.

Harshal: glad, lover.

Harshaman: full of joy, delighted.

Harhamay: essence of joy.

Harshan: causing delight.

Harshendu: moon of joy.

Harshi: pleased, joyful.

Harshit: full of joy.

Harshod: creating joy.

Harshul: cheerful, deer, lover.

Harshvardhan: one who increases joy, happiness.

Haryaksh: yellow-eyed, lion.

Haryalā: precious, desired, pleasant, deer.

Haseen: handsome.

Hasit: delighting, delighted.

Hassan: saint.

Hāssan: handsome boy.

Hatakesh: lord of gold, Shiva.

Hātakeshwar: lord of gold, Shiva.

Hatish: desireless.

Hatitosh: not afraid of troubles.

Havan: invocation, sacrifice, calling.

Havighna: sacrificial.

Havirdhan: with sacrifice as one's wealth.

Havishman: sacrificial.

Havishmat: believing in sacrifices.

Hayagreev: with a horse's neck.

Heenadosh: faultless.

Heera: quintessence, diamond, lion, thunderbolt.

Heerak: diamond.

Heeral: bearer of diamonds.

Heeren: lord of gems, attractive pearls.

Heeresh: king of gems.

Heeru: hard as diamonds.

Heli: embrace, all-pervasive sun.

Hemabal: gold power, pearl.

Hemabhojam: golden lotus.

Hemachandra: golden moon.

Hemādri: golden mountain.

Hemakānt: as bright as gold.

Hemakeshi: golden-haired, Shiva.

Hemāl: lamb.

Heman: golden yellow, golden, jasmine, saffron, gold ornament.

Hemanāth: lord of gold, Shiva.

Hemāng: golden-bodied, lion, Vishnu, Brahma.

Hemant: winter.

Hemanya: gold-bodied.

Hemaprakash: golden light.

Hemarāj: lord of gold.

Hemashankh: with a golden conchshell.

Hemashikh: gold-crested.

Hemavatinandan: son of Goddess Parvati (Ganesh) .

Hemendra: lord of gold.

Hemendu: golden moon.

Hemenshu: moon.

Heramba: boastful, name of Ganapati.

Herman: warrior.

Heti: flame.

Himādri: peak of snow.

Himadyuti: cool radiance, moon.

Himakar: snow-handed, causing cold, white, moon.

Himakiran: cold-rayed, moon.

Himambu: snow-water, dew.

Himānhu: cool-rayed, moon.

Himanshu: one radiating cool light (moon).

Himashaila: snow mountain.

Himavān: cold, of white, having snow.

Himoshra: white-rayed.

Hinkar: chanting of hymns, invocation of a deity.

Hiranchay: deer-footed.

Hirang: diamond-bodied, as hard as diamond.

Hiranya: gold, most precious, Vishnu.

Hirañyaksha: golden-eyed.

Hiranyamay: full of gold.

Hiranyav: golden ornament, property of a God.

Hiren: lord of gems, beautiful pearls.

Hiresh: king of Gems.

Hirishipra: golden-checked.

Hitaishi: well-wisher.

Hiteshin: benevolent.

Hiteshwar: God of welfare, caring for others.

Honna: to possess.

Hoshang: to be one's own self.

Homa: oblation.

Hresha: delighted.

Hridyesha: Lord of the heart.

Hrim: wealth.

Howarḍ: guardian of home.

Hridayesh: king of Heart.

Hrideek: of heart, friendship.

Hridesh: beloved.

Hridyānand: joy of the heart.

Hridyanāt: lord of the heart.

Hridyanshu: light from heart, moon.

Hrishikesh: controller of senses, lord Krishna, lord Vishnu.

Hugh: bright in mind and spirit.

Hukum: order.

Hussain: handsome.

Hrisada: noise.

Hrishikesha: Lord Krishna.

Hreidi: heart.

Hurditya: very happy.

I

Iāgo: supplanter, representative.

Ian: God's gracious gift.

Ibhān: elephant-faced, Ganesha.

Ibhānan: elephant-faced, Ganesha.

Ibrāhim: father of many.

Iḍā: stream of praise, time period.

Iddham: shining, blazing, glowing, heat, light, sunshine.

Idhānt: bright, pure, resplendent.

Idrees: father of many, enthusiastic prince.

Idwal: prince of the Wall.

Ignatius: fiery.

Igor: army warrior with a bow.

Ihsān: beneficence.

Ijya: worthy of worship.

Ikshan̄: sight.

Ikshud: sweetness-giver, sweet-tongued.

Ikshvāku: desire-attracter.

Ikvāl: prosperity, good fortune.

Ilāchandra: moon of the earth.

Ilādhar: holder of the earth, mountain.

Ilāhi: term of an era begun by Akbar.

Ilānko: surface of the earth.

Ilāsh: God.

Ilāspati: lord of the earth.

Ilavil: protector of the earth.

Ilavrit: protector of speech.

Ilesh: lord of earth.

Ilila: having high intelligence.

Ilūkh: convering the earth, wanderer.

Ilyās: a prophet's name.

Imād: support.

Immanuel: God is with us.

Imrān: a prophet's name.

Imtiyāz: great king.

Inakānt: beloved of the sun.

Inan: sun, king, lord, master.

Inas: able, bold, glorious, mighty, powerful, strong, wild.

Inās: capable.

Ināyat: benevolence.

Indeevar: best among the precious, blessing, blue lotus.

Indeshwar: lord of the moon.

Indra: god of sky, god of atmosphere, excellent, chief, first, sign of generous heroism.

Indradutt: gift of Lord Indra.

Indragiri: mountain of Indra.

Indraguru: teacher of Indra.

Indraj: born of Indra.

Indrajit: conqueror of Indra.

Indraneel: as blue as Indra, sapphire.

Indrapālit: protected by Indra.

Indrāsan: throne of Indra.

Indratan: as strong as Indra.

Indresit: sent by Indra.

Indubhushan: moon, Shiva.

Indugiri: mountain of the moon, cool, fair, silver, soothing.

Induj: mercury (planet).

Indukamal: moon-like lotus, white lotus.

Indukānt: beloved of the moon, moonstone.

Indukar: hand of the moon, moonbeam.

Indupāl: gem of the moon, moonstone, ocean.

Indushekhar: lord Shiva, lord Vishnu.

Inesh: strong king, Vishnu.

Inganam: knowledge.

Ingram: raven.

Inoday: sunrise.

Inukānt: beloved of the sun.

Intazār: hope.

Irā: watchful, descendant.

Iraish: lord of the earth, Vishnu, Ganesha.

Irajā: born of the wind, Hanuman.

Irām: shining.

Irāvaj: born of the water, lotus.

Irāvān: having water or milk, ocean, cloud, king.

Irāvat: laden with water, cloud.

Ireesh: lord of the earth, Vishnu, Ganesha.

Irfān: thankfulness, gratitude.

Irith: of wind, perfume.

Irma: of wind's nature, ever-moving, instigating everything.

Irshad: sign.

Irving: handsome, fair.

Irwin: wid boar, friend.

Irya: powerful, active, energetic.

Isaac: he who laughs.

Isha: God, lord of the universe, fertile,pious, powerful, all-pervading, swift, venerated, divine, Shiva.

Ishan: bestowing wealth.

Ishān: lord, sovereign, safeguard Vishnu, Shiva.

Ishānam: light, splendour.

Ishāq: a prophet's name.

Ishat: greatness, superiority.

Ishayu: fresh, powerful, strong.

Ishik: desirable, silk cotton tree.

Ishir: active, powerful, guide, refreshing, strong.

Ishit: desired.

Ishmin: as swift as spring, fast, impetuous, like the wind.

Ishrit: owner, master, lord of the universe.

Ishu: quivering, arrow, ray of light.

Ishuka: arrow.

Ishva: spiritual teacher.

Ishvas: archer.

Ishwar: powerful, the supreme God.

Ishya: spring season.

Ismāil: God will hear.

Isrā: freedom.

Itant: shining, bright, clean, sharp, wonderful.

Itar: another.

Itish: lord.

Itur: perfume.

Ivan: God is gracious.

Iveelak: wealthy son.

Ives: little archer.

Ivor: army warrior.

Izekiel: strength of God.

J

Jabāli: goatherd.

Jabbar: barley grower, peasant.

Jabir: comforter.

Jagad: universe, world.

Jagadānand: delight of the universe, pleasing the world.

Jagadātman: soul of the universe, Supreme Spirit.

Jagadāy: life of the universe, wind.

Jagadeep: light of the world.

Jagadguru: preceptor of the universe, Brahma, Vishnu, Shiva, Rama.

Jagadeesh: lord of the universe, Brahma.

Jagajeet: conquerer of the world.

Jagajeevan: life of the world, worldly life.

Jagamohan: one who attracts the world (Jagatmohan).

Jagan: world, universe.

Jagānant: to whom the world belongs.

Jaganarayan: god of the world (Jagatnarayan).

Jagandeep: lamp of the universe, creator of the universe, Brahma.

Jagannath: lord of the world.

Jaganu: living being, fire.

Jāgar: armour.

Jagat: alive, moving, world, people.

Jagatbehari: world traveler (Jagvihari).

Jagati: endowed with speed.

Jagatidhar: earth-supporter, mountain.

Jagatkishor: world child.

Jagatpal: caretaker of the world (God).

Jagatprabhu: god of the world.

Jagatprakash: light of the world.

Jagavant: owner of the world.

Jagatveer: bravest in the world (Jagveer).

Jagesh: lord of the world.

Jagmi: world-pervading, wind.

Jagnesh: Shiva.

Jagnu: carrier of the world, fire.

Jāgravi: waterful, bright, sun.

Jaguri: awakener, one who has risen up, leader, conductor.

Jahnu: ear, good listener, Vishnu.

Jai: conqueror, victor, flute, sun.

Jaichandra: moon among victors, ever victorious.

Jaidev: lord of victory.

Jaidhar: bearer of victory.

Jaijan: victory.

Jaikar: mine of victory.

Jaikrit: causing victory.

Jaimān: victorious.

Jaipāl: guardian of victory, king.

Jairāj: victorious ruler.

Jaisheesh: cheer of victory, victorious head, best among victors.

Jaishnav: desirous of victory.

Jaitang: one who has mastered one's senses, beyond worldly attachments.

Jaivant: long-lived.

Jaivat: being victorious, winning.

Jājhar: very powerful, warrior.

Jalādhip: lord of the waters.

Jalaj: water-born, lotus, conchshell, moon.

Jalakarank: enveloped by water, born in water, conchshell, lotus, cloud, wave.

Jalāmbar: water-clad, ocean.

Jalanchal: water-clad, spring, fountain.

Jalaneel: blue colour of water.

Jalāntak: containing water.

Jalas: water-like, appearing, happiness, healing.

Jalasandh: confluence of waters.

Jalāshay: reposing on water, pond, Vishnu.

Jalbhushan: ornament of water (means wind).

Jaldev: god of water (Lord-Varun).

Jaldhar: one who holds water (meaning cloud).

Jaleel: great.

Jalendra: lord of the waters.

Jalendu: reflection of the moon in water.

Jalesh: ocean.

Jalit: radiance, influence.

Jamāl: beauty.

Jamālin: connoisseur.

Jambuki: purple, indigo, amethyst.

Jameel: good looking.

Janachandra: moon among people.

Janādhip: lord of men.

Janak: father of Sita according to Ramayana, creator.

Janakibhushan: ornament of Janki (Lord Rama).

Janakinath: lord Rama.

Janakiraman: lord Rama.

Janamejay: victorious from birth, causing men to tremble.

Janapadin: ruler of a country, king.

Janapālak: protector of men.

Janārdhan: exciting people, Vishnu, Krishna.

Janashrut: famous among people.

Janāv: protecting people.

Janesh: lord of men, king.

Jangari: swift, fast.

Jangi: warrior.

Janishṭa: desired by people.

Janit: born.

Janu: soul.

Janya: born.

Janyu: born, creature, fire, Brahma.

Japendu: lord Shiva.

Japesh: lord of chanters, lord Shiva.

Jaritari: enemy of old age.

Jaritri: singer of hymns, invoker, worshipper.

Jarūu: waving, moon.

Jārvis: driver.

Jasalin: abode of fame.

Jasamit: extremely famous.

Jasapāl: protected by fame.

Jasapreet: desiring fame.

Jasarāj: lord of fame.

Jasavant: having fame.

Jashan: merriment, festival.

Jashank: cupid.

Jasveer: hero of fame, victorious.

Jaswant: victorious (Yashwant).

Jatilesh: Shiva.

Jatin: having twisted hair, bearing the lineage.

Javāhar: jewel.

Javan: swift.

Javanil: swift mind, hurricane.

Javas: efficient.

Javin: swift, deer, horse.

Jawahar: jewel

Jay: victory.

Jayachand: victory moon.

Jayadeep: light of victory.

Jayaditya: victorious sun.

Jay āneek: army of victors.

Jayant: victorious finally, moon, Vishnu, Shiva.

Jayapal: king, Lord Vishnu, Lord Bramha.

Jayaprakash: light of victory.

Jayarat: immersed in victory.

Jayashekhar: crest of victory.

Jayāshnav: taster of victory.

Jayawant: victorious.

Jayendra: lord of victory.

Jayin: conqueror.

Jaysukh: pleasure of victory.

Jed: hand.

Jeeva: living being, alive personal soul, principle of life, earth.

Jeevaj: born alive.

Jeevan: life, giving life, son, wind sun, Shiva.

Jeevanprakash: light of life.

Jeevant: long-lived.

Jeevarāj: lord of life.

Jeevat: spirited, courageous, bold.

Jeevesh: God.

Jeevitesh: lord of the living, sun, moon.

Jeman: having victory, victor.

Jenya: of noble origin, true.

Jetva: to be gained.

Jibril: archangel.

Jina: victor.

Jinendra: lord of life.

Jishnu: triumphant, Arjun.

Jitamanyu: conqueror of anger.

Jitendra: conqueror of senses.

Jivesh: Almighty.

Jogendra: king of ascetics, Shiva.

Jogesh: lord of ascetics, Shiva.

Jogia: saffron colour (worn by ascetics).

Jogindra: lord Shiva.

Jograj: Yograj, king of Yoga, Lord Krishna.

Jāgara: armoor.

Jāhusha: young animal.

Johar: precious stone.

Josh: approval, bud, pleasure, satisfaction.

Joshit: pleased.

Joting: absorbed in penance.

Jūvas: quickness.

Jwāla: flame, blaze, light, shine, torchglow.

Jwalaprasad: gift of flame.

Jyamagh: great, superior, winning battles.

Jyāyas: greater, stronger, superior.

Jyotiprakash: light of flame.

Jyotiranjan: happy flame.

Jyotirdhar: one who holds the flame, sun.

Jyotirmay: consisting of light, Vishnu, Shiva.

Jyotish: luminous, full of light, fire, sun.

Jyotishk: luminous.

Jyotishmān: possessor of light.

Jyāyoo: stronger.

Jushta: loved.

K

Kāchin: abode of clouds, tree.

Kadin: friend.

Kāgni: small fire.

Kāhali: mishievous, Shiva.

Kāhol: bringing water, drinking water.

Kailāsh: mountain in the Himalayan range, mountain where Shiva dwells.

Kailasnath, Kailashnath: lord of mount Kailash (i.e Lord Shiva).

Kairav: water-born, white lotus.

Kaishik: hairlike, fine as hair, love, passion.

Kaivalya: emancipation, bliss.

Kākand: gold.

Kakshak: living in the forest.

Kakshap: water-drinker.

Kaladhar: one who shows different phases (i.e. the moon).

Kalanath: moon.

Kalanidhi: moon, Lord Shiva.

Kālanjay: conqueror of time, conqueror of death, Krishna.

Kalāp: intelligent, quiver of arrows, peacock's tail, ornament, totality.

Kalāpak: with feathers, with skills, band, bundle, ornament, peacock, single string of pearls, quiver of arrows, moon.

Kalāpin: peacock, Indian cuckoo.

Kālāri: enemy of death, Krishna.

Kalash: pitcher, churn, temple top.

Kalāvak: sparrow.

Kalesh: Shiva.

Kalhar: water lily.

Kalicharan: feet of Goddess Kali (Goddess Durga).

Kalidas: devotee of Godess Kali, name of a famous poet of India.

Kalijan: men of art, skilled men, auspicious, blessed, beautiful, excellent, fortunate, happy.

Kālik: beyond death, long-lived.

Kalil: deep, not perceivable.

Kalind: bestower of arts and skills, blossom-giver, sun.

Kaling: knower of arts and skills, pervader of blossom.

Kalit: known, understood.

Kaliki: destroyer of sins, tenth incarnation of Vishnu.

Kālkrit: decided by time, constant, peacock, sun.

Kallol: joy, huge wave, surge, happiness, pleasure.

Kalmali: dispeller of darkness, brightness, splendour.

Kalmash: dotted with black, variegated.

Kalpa: fit, able, competent, proper, grants wishes, ritual, opinion, determination.

Kalpak: of a particular norm, rite, ceremony.

Kalpanāth: lord of time, lord of perfection.

Kalparat: as perfect as time, perfect.

Kalpesh: lord of perfection.

Kalpit: imagined, fit, proper.

Kalvik: sparrow.

Kālya: timely, agreeable, auspicious, pleasant.

Kalyān: welfare, agreeable, beneficial, excellent, beautiful, fortunate, virtuous, propitious.

Kalyanin: happy, auspicious, beneficial, illustrious, fortunate, prosperous, virtuous.

Kamadev: god of love (lust), Cupid.

Kamal: lotus, pale red, rose-hued, Brahma.

Kamalāhās: smiling like a lotus.

Kamalaj: lotus-born, Brahma.

Kamalākar: cluster of lotuses.

Kamalaksh: lotus-eyed.

Kamalamay: consisting of lotuses.

Kamalanayan: lotus-eyed.

Kamalāsan: with lotus as seat.

Kamalbandhu: friend or brother of lotus (sun).

Kamalesh, Kamaleshwar: god of lotus (Lord Vishnu) (Kamaleshwar).

Kamalkant: lord Vishnu.

Kamalnath: lord Vishnu.

Kāmat: following one's desires, unrestrained.

Kambar: of variegated hues.

Kamboj: shell, elephant.

Kāmik: desired, wished for.

Kamil: protection.

Kamineesh: ruling the God of love.

Kamlapati: lord Vishnu.

Kāmod: granter of wishes.

Kanak: gold, sandalwood, thornapple.

Kanakādri: golden mountain.

Kanakamay; consisting of gold, golden.

Kanakendu: golden moon.

Kanal: shining, bright.

Kanan: forest.

Kanav: able, expert, honoured, appreciated, wise.

Kānchan: shining, gold, wealth.

Kanchār: shining, sun.

Kandan: knower, camphor, cloud, garlic, radish.

Kānha: adolescent, Krishna.

Kanhaiya: adolescent, Krishna.

Kanik: grain, corn ear, atom, core of wheat.

Kanishka: small.

Kanjak: water and earth born.

Kanjam: ambrosia, nectar, lotus.

Kanjār: sun, elephant, peacock, hermit, belly, Brahma.

Kanka: lotus fragrance, heron.

Kanthamani: necklace jewel.

Kañva: talented, louded, respected, honoured, intelligent.

Kañval: lotus.

Kanvar: prince.

Kapaali: lord Shiva.

Kapi: monkey, sun.

Kapidhwaj: one with monkey flag (Arjun).

Kapil: monkey-coloured, tawny, brown, reddish, sun, Vishnu, Shiva.

Kapil: white innocent, lord Shiva.

Kapilashwa: one with a white horse (Lord Indra).

Kapindra: king of monkeys (Hanuman, Sugreev).

Kapirath: one with monkey or sun on his chariot (Lord Rama/Arjun).

Kapish: lord of monkeys, raddish-brown, brown, incense, sun, Shiva.

Kaprith: increasing pleasure.

Karam: deeds.

Kardal: mustard.

Kārin: doing, jubliant, accomplishing, praising, rejoicing.

Karmañya: clever in work, skilful, diligent.

Karna, Karan: eldest brother of Pandavas, ear.

Karña: ear, skilful, clever, adroit, Supreme Being, field, ship's rudder, document.

Karnabhushan: ear ring, ear ornament.

Karnajeet: conquerer of Karna (i.e. Arjun).

Karnapriya: something that is sweet to our ears.

Karshin: one who attracts.

Kartār: lord of all creation.

K ārtik: bestower of courage and happiness.

Kartikeya: god of war, one born in month of Kartik or Kritika nakshatra.

Karuñ: compassionate, tender, Supreme Being.

Karunakar: very kind.

Karunanidhi: one whose heart is full of kindness.

Karunesh: lord of mercy, moon.

Kāsha: appearance.

Kāshagesh: sugarcane.

Kāsār: pond.

Kashik: shining one.

Kāshin: shining, conqueror-like appearance.

Kashinath: lord of Kashi (Varanasi), lord Shiva.

Kastur: musk.

Katam: best, very handsome.

Kāteb: writer.

Katith: praised by all, well recited.

Kātyāyan: desirer.

Kauleen: from a noble family.

Kausha: silken, skill.

Kaushal: well-being, welfare, happiness, prosperity.

Kaushik: knower of hidden treasure, owl, sheathed, snake-catcher, sentiment of love, Shiva, Arabian jasmine.

Kaushtubh: heavenly jewel.

Kavan: water.

Kavash: shield.

Kaveesh: lord of poets, best physician.

Kavela: water-born, lotus.

Kavi: poet, omniscient, clever, physician, sensible, singer, surgeon, Brahma, sun.

Kavindra: prince among poets.

Kavindu: moon among poets.

Kavitar: great poet.

Kāvya: poem, with qualities of poet or sage, inspired, intelligence, prophetic, wisdom.

Kedār: meadow, field.

Kedarnath: lord of mount Kedar (Lord Shiva).

Keela: flame.

Keeli: parrot.

Keenāsh: cultivator of soil, ploughman.

Keertan: praise, praising, respecting, devotional song.

Keertimān: famous.

Keertimant: famous.

Keertimay: consisting of fame, famous.

Keertit: famous, celebrated.

Kegan: fiery.

Keith: wood, wind, wood-dweller.

Kekāval: peacock.

Kekay: full of water, place having water sources.

Kelas: crystal.

Kelik: sportive, sporting.

Kelvin: a river.

Kenneth: handsome, fire-born, royal oath.

Kenṭ: border, coast, bright white.

Kesar: hair of the brow, mane, saffron.

Keshav: long-haired, slayer of demon Keshi, Vishṇu, Krishna.

Keshavar: with beautiful hair, saffron.

Ketak: flat, banner, gold ornament for hair.

Ketan: house, banner, flag-invitation, sign, symbol.

Ketubh: cloud.

Keval: pure, excellent, good,

Kevalin: seeker of the Absolute.

Keya: speed.

Keyūr: armlet.

Khadir: celestial, heavenly.

Khadyot: firefly, sun.

Khagañ: moving through space.

Khaganj: best among birds.

Khagendra: king of birds, eagle (Garuda).

Khagesh: lord of birds.

Khajit: conquering heaven.

Khālid: immortal.

Khanak: digger, miner.

Khañḍav: sweetmeat, candy, sugar.

Khanjan: dimple, bird.

Khapūr: full of space, filler of skies, betelnut tree.

Kharānshu: sharp-rayed, sun.

Khilāvan: a player in the sky, arrow, sun.

Khushil: happy, pleasant.

Khushman: with a happy mind.

Khushwant: one full of happiness.

Khyān: knowledge, preception.

Khyāt: pervading the sky, named, called, celebrated.

Kilal: nectar, wine.

Kim: chief.

Kindam: conqueror of the proud.

Kinjat: blossom.

Kiṅkan: lotus bud, bell.

Kimishuk: a very small parrot, parrot-shaped, odourless.

Kipling: one who cures.

Kiran: ray.

Kiraṇ: dust, small, particle of dust, ray, beam of light, sunbeam, moonbeam.

Kiraṇmay: full of rays.

Kireeṭ: crown, diadem, tiara, crest.

Kirik: sparkling, beaming.

Kirin: appreciator, poet, author, orator.

Kiritmani: jewel in the crown.

Kirmeer: of different hues.

Kirtan: devotional song.

Kirti: fame.

Kirtibhushan: one adorned with fame.

Kirtivallabh: aspirant of fame.

Kishor: adolescent, colt, youth, sun, Krishna.

Kokil: firebrand, Indian cuckoo.

Komal: delicate, beautiful, soft, tender, sweet, handsome.

Kopal: tender shoot of plant.

Koteesh: lord of millions.

Kovid: wise, knowledgeable.

Kripa: beauty, appearance, compassion, favour, kindness, splendour, tenderness.

Kripāl: gentle, kind.

Kripānand: pleaser with kindness.

Kripāneel: living in splendour.

Kripanidhi: one with heart full of mercy.

Kripāsāgar: ocean of compassion.

Krisha: lean.

Krishaṅin: decorated with pearls.

Krishna: black, dark blue, Vishnu's incarnation.

Krishnamoorti: idol of Lord Krishna.

Kritagya: grateful.

Kriti: creation, Vishnu.

Kritimān: creator, sculptor.

Kritin: active, blessed, clever, happy, learned, expert, lucky, pure, pious, skilful, satisfied, successful, virtuous, wise.

Kritya: action, achievement.

Kshamak: merciful.

Kshaman: soil, earth, ground.

Kshem: welfare, bless, emancipation, peace, safety, security, welfare, tranquillity.

Kshipra: elastic, quick, speedy, springing.

Kshiraj: moon, lotus, conch -shell.

Kshitidhar: mountain.

Kshitij: son of the earth, snail, earthworm, horizon, tree.

Kshitish: lord of earth.

Kuldeep: heir to the family.

Kuldev: family diety.

Kulik: well-born.

Kuleen: high-born, of a noble family.

Kulvir: hero of the family.

Kumār: child, boy, youth, prince.

Kumāresh: lord of youths.

Kumāril: intelligent youth.

Kumud: pleasure of the earth, white water lily, red lotus, camphor, Vishnu.

Kumudesh: lord of white water lily, moon.

Kunadik: pleaser of earth.

Kunāl: lotus.

Kundra: musk, jasmine, oleander, Vishnu.

Kundan: pure, fine, glittering, gold, purified, sparkling.

Kunind: administrator.

Kunjabehari: one who roams in kunja (i.e Lord Krishna).

Kunjal: living in shrubs, Indian cuckoo.

Kunjalik: lotus.

Kunjar: residing in forests, elephant.

Kunsh: shine, speak.

Kunwar: a prince.

Kupat: excellent.

Kurchik: painter's brush.

Kushal: bringer of sacred grass, auspicious, clever, efficient, good, happy, skilled, proper, plan.

Kustubh: sea, ocean, Vishnu.

Kushika: one who is squint.

Kushilava: singer.

Kushin: furnished with kusha grass.

Kushtnā: abode on earth.

Kusmilā: filled with flowers.

Kusumbha: sunflower.

Kusumeshu: arrow of flowers.

Kutsa: thunderbolt.

Kusumākar: treasure of flowers, garden, spring season.

Kuva: enricher of knowledge, water lily.

Kuvam: producer of earth, sun.

Kuvar: astringent in flavour, fragrant.

Kuvala: water lily pearl.

Kuvam: one who produce earth.

Kuvara: fragrant.

Kuvayu: causing a bad harvest.

Kuvana: a tinkle.

Kunjitā: hidden in forest.

Kurottam: best of Kurus.

Kuranga: a deer.

L

Laghat: wind.

Laghu: light, low, lovely, gentle, pure soft, small, swift, subtle, young.

Lājawān: modest, shy.

Lajit: modest, shy.

Laksh: aim, objective.

Lakshak: ray of beauty.

Lakshan̄: with an auspicious mark.

Lakshang: one with auspicious mark.

Lakshman̄: with auspicious marks, target achiever, fortunate.

Lakshmikant: husband of Lakshmi (Lord Vishnu), or a rich person.

Lakshminarayan: Lakshmi and Lord Vishnu together.

Lakshminath: lord Vishnu.

Lakshmipati: husband of Lakshmi (Lord Vishnu).

Lakshmiraman: lord Vishnu.

Lākulesh: God.

Lāl: precious stone.

Lalchand, Lalchandra: red moon.

Lālil: beautiful, affectionately tended.

Lalit: handsome, lovely.

Lalitāditya: beautiful sun.

Lalitchandra: a beautiful moon.

Lalitesh: god of beauty, husband of a beautiful wife.

Lalitlochan: one with beautiful eyes.

Lalitmohan: beautiful & attractive.

Lalitya: good-looking. affectionate.

Lamak: lover, chivalrous person.

Lamban: great, large, tall, spacious, long necklace, Shiva.

Lambit: procured, cherished.

Lanḍer: property owner.

Lāshak: dancer, peacock, frolicker, Shiva.

Lashit: wished, yearned for.

Lauhit: made of metal, red.

Lava: tiny, piece, particle.

Lavam: small, clove.

Lavaṅ: handsome, lovely, salt.

Lavaṅik: handsome, beautiful, saline.

Lavaneesh: lord of the sea.

Lāvaṅya: beautiful, lustrous.

Lavitra: subtle one, Shiva.

Lawson: son of Lawrence.

Laya: deep concentration, rest, fusion, Supreme Being.

Leon: lion.

Levin: lightning.

Likhit: written.

Lincoln: home by the pond.

Linḍsay: pool island.

Lābha: profit.

Lāsya: a dance.

Lipshit: desired.

Loban: incense.

Lochan: eye.

Lohit: red, copper.

Lohitashwa: one with red horse (Lord Shiva), Fire.

Lokātman: soul of the universe.

Lokbhushan: ornament of the world.

Lokesh: lord of the world, Brahma.

Loknath: lord of all worlds, king.

Lokpradeep: Gautam Budha.

Lokprakash: light of the world.

Lomesh: ancient sage's name.

Lowell: beloved.

Loyin: beauty.

Lynḍon: linden tree.

Laghuga: moving fast.

Lomasa: hairy.

M

Mada: intoxication, ecstasy, honey, hilarity, wine, musk, pride, passion.

Madan: passion, love, intoxicating, exhilirating, delighting, spring.

Madangopal: lovely cowherd (Lord Krishna).

Madanmohan: lovely & attractive (Lord Krishna).

Madesh: lord of intoxication, Shiva.

Mādhav: vernal, relating to spring season, Shiva, Krishna.

Madhu: sweet, charming, delightful, delicious, honey nectar, sugar, wine.

Madhughosh: sweet sounding.

Madhuj: made of honey, sugar.

Madhukant: moon.

Madhukar: large black bee.

Madhukosh: honeycomb.

Madhul: sweet, intoxicating drink.

Madhumay: consisting of honey.

Madhup: bee.

Madhur: sweet, pleasant, charming, delightful, melodious.

Madhusudhana: lord Krishna, one who killed demon Madhu, bee.

Mādhva: born of the spring, born of honey, beautiful, intoxicating.

Madin: delightful, exhilirating, intoxicating, lovely.

Madoodan: beautiful garden.

Madur: bird.

Magan: absorbed, engrossed.

Magaran: following a path, wind.

Maghavan: generous, beautiful, liberal.

Mahabahu: one with strong arms (Arjun).

Mahabali: strong, one with great strength.

Mahādev: Shiva.

Mahaj: high-born, of noble descent.

Mahajay: extremely victorious.

Mahakant: very pleasing, Shiva.

Mahaksh: large-eyed, Shiva.

Mahamati: one with big brain (Ganesh).

Mahānand: highest bliss.

Mahānt: great.

Mahārt: very truthful.

Mahāswin: brilliant, glorious, splendour.

Mahavir: most courageous amongst men.

Maheej: son of the earth.

Maheep: protector of the earth, king.

Maheepati: the king.

Mahipati: king.

Mahendra: Vishnu.

Mahesh: great lord, God.

Maheshkumar: son of Lord Shiva (Ganesh, Kartikey).

Maheshu: great arrow.

Maheshwar: lord Shiva.

Māhi: earth.

Mahidās: devotee of the earth.

Mahikānshu: with frosty rays, moon.

Mahiman: greatness, power, dignity, might.

Māhin: giving delight, joyous, exalted, great, mighty.

Māhipāl: king.

Mahipati: king.

Māhir: expert, proficient.

Mahish: mighty, great, lord of the earth, buffalo, sun.

Mahit: celebrated, honoured.

Māhiyu: joyful, delighted.

Mahoday: greatly risen, eminent, honoured.

Mahtāb: moon, moonlight.

Mahu; diver-bird, war-vessel.

Mahua: highly honoured.

Māhyā: one who is honoured.

Mainda: giver of art.

Maitra: friendly, amicable, kind.

Maitreya: friendly, benevolent.

Majeed: worthy of worship.

Makarand: honey, nectar.

Makhesh: lord of sacrifice.

Makul: bud.

Malay: fragrant, sandalwood tree.

Malhār: rain-giver.

Māli: fragrant.

Mālidev: god of fragrance.

Mālik: master.

Māhin: garlanded, gardener, florist, crowned.

Mālkosh: musical mode.

Mallārjun: handsome wrestler.

Mallesh: lord of wrestless, Shiva.

Malhi: possessing, holding, jasmine.

Mālyavān: garland bearer, one who is crowned.

Mālyovan: rich, wealthy.

Māmti: affectionate, loving.

Manahar: winning the heart, charming, attractive, fascinating.

Manaj: mind-born.

Manakānt: dear to the mind.

Manakar: fulfiller of wishes.

Manal: bird.

Manan: meditation, intelligence, reflection, thought, understanding.

Manāp: giving the heart, beautiful, attractive.

Manas: intellect, intelligence, perception.

Mānas: mind-conceived, soul, spiritual mind, mental powers.

Mānav: lad, youth, pearl ornament.

Manavendra: king.

Manāyu: zealous, devoted.

Manchit: desired.

Mandanum: praise.

Mandār: large, firm, slow, thick, pearl chain.

Mandayu: cheerful, gay, happy.

Mandeep: lamp of mind.

Māndhan: rich in honour.

Mandhatri: prince.

Mandin: delighting, exhilirating.

Mandit: adorned, decorated.

Mandu: pleased, joyful, cheerful.

Maneech: flower, hand, pearl.

Maneesh: lord of the mind.

Maneesin: thoughtful, intelligent, devout, prudent, wise.

Maneesit: desired, wished.

Manendra: lord of the soul.

Manendra: king of mind.

Mangal: auspiciousness, bless, felicity, happiness, welfare.

Mañgalya: pure, pious, beautiful, gold, luck-bringer, sandalwood, woodapple.

Mangesh: lord Shiva.

Manharan: gift.

Manhaṭtan: whiskey.

Mani: gem.

Māniar: beautiful, pleasant, attractive.

Manibhushan: an ornament of jewels, very best jewel.

Manidhar: a mythical snake with jewel in its hood.

Mānik: highly honoured.

Manik: jewel, gem.

Manikam: collyrium.

Mānikya: ruby.

Manimān: jewelled, sun.

Manimat: adorned with jewels.

Manimay: made of jewels.

Maninder: king among jewels, diamond.

Manindra: diamond, lord of mind.

Manirāg: jewel-coloured.

Manirāj: king of jewels, diamond.

Maniram: jewel of a person.

Manisar: string of jewels, jewelled necklace.

Manish: intelligent, God of mind.

Manishankar: lord Shiva.

Manishyām: emerald.

Manit: honoured, respected, notable, known.

Manivar: best jewel, diamond.

Manjav: swift as thought.

Manjeet: winner of mind.

Manjendra: king.

Manjir: cymbal, anklet.

Manjudev: lord of beauty.

Manjughosh: sweet sounding recitation.

Manjul: beautiful.

Manjunāth: lord of beauty, lord of ice, Shiva.

Manjuprān: beautiful soul, Brahma.

Manjushak: celestial flower.

Manjushree: divine beauty.

Manksha: longing, yearning, desire.

Mankur: reflector of mind, mirror.

Manmit: heart, selected.

Manmohan: one who attacts mind.

Mannat: with a devoted mind.

Manodatta: mind-given.

Manohar: winning the heart, heart-stealer, jasmine, Krishna.

Manohar: one who wins over minds, atteractive.

Manoj: mind-born, love, Krishna.

Manoneet: carried by the mind, approved, chosen.

Manoranjan: one who pleases the mind.

Manot: mind-born.

Manprasad: mentally calm & cool person.

Manshesht: Vishnu.

Mānsij: cupid.

Mansukh: pleasure of mind.

Mansūr: divinely aided.

Manta: thought.

Mantu: advisor, man, arbiter, ruler.

Manu: soul.

Manug: follower of wishes.

Manurāj: king of men.

Manyu: anger, mind, mood, passion, rage, temper, zeal.

Manyumat: ardent, spirited, passionate, vehement.

Mārachitta: destroyer of desires.

Marakat: emerald.

Maral: rock-born, born to Shiva's blessings, duck.

Marāl: mild, soft, tender.

Marand: nectar.

Marānk: marked by love.

Mardan: crushing, grinding.

Markandeya: a sage.

Mārshal: horse groomer.

Martānd: sun.

Māreech: glowing.

Māreechimat: radiant, with rays, shining, sun.

Mārgin: pioneer, guide.

Mārgit: sought, desired, needed.

Māris: worthy, respectable.

Mārmik: with deep unsight, knowing the essence, perceptive, very intelligent.

Mārmit: destroyer of Kama, Shiva.

Mārshak: very respectable, honourable.

Martand: sun.

Maru: desert, rock, mountain.

Marūk: antelope, deer, peacock, from wildness.

Marut: air, breath, breeze, wind, shining one.

Mārut: breath, air, wind, belonging to the wind, Vishnu.

Maruti: Hanuman, Bhimsen

Mārvin: beautiful sea, good friend.

Mashāl: torch.

Masār: emerald, sapphire.

Mātang: wandering at will, cloud, elephant, best of its kind.

Matil: intelligent.

Matimat: wise.

Matinār: possessing intellect.

Matsendra: king of the fishes.

Mauli: chief, head, best, crown, diadem, foremost.

Maxwell: from the great well.

Māyañ: detached from wealth.

Mayank: marked like a deer, moon.

Mayas: delight, enjoyment, pleasure, refreshment.

Māyin: illusionary, skilled in enchanting, Brahma, Shiva.

Mayresh: Ganesh.

Māyukh: ray of light, flame, lustre, brightness.

Mayūr: peacock, celery.

Mechak: gem, cloud, deep blue.

Medhājit: victor of intelligence.

Medhas: sacrifice.

Medhāvi: wise, intelligent.

Medhir: wise, intelligent.

Medineesh: lord of the earth, king.

Meedush: generous.

Megh: cloud, sprinkler, mass.

Meghadeep: light of the cloud, lightning.

Meghānand: rejoining in clouds, peacocks.

Meghaneel: blue cloud.

Megharāj: lord of clouds, Vishnu.

Meghdutt: gift of clouds.

Meghnad: thunder.

Mehtāb: moon.

Mehul: rain.

Mekal: knower of the self.

Melville: hillside, town by the mill.

Melvin: servant.

Menādhav: lover of intellect.

Merlin: sea, falcon.

Meva: praise, worship.

Midhush: abundance.

Mihikanshee: mist-rayed, moon.

Mihir: causing heat-light-rain, sun, air, cloud, wind, sage.

Mihirkiran: sun ray.

Milind: wanting an encounter, bee encountering flower.

Milṭon: from the mill town.

Mirang: coral.

Mitesh: one with few desires.

Mithil: kingdom.

Mithilesh: Lord of Mithila (Sitạs father).

Mithun: forming a pair, honey, clarified butter.

Mitul: limited, measured, moderate.

Mohan: beautiful, infatuating, Shiva, Krishna.

Mohin: attractive.

Mohit: infatuated, bewitched, love-intoxicated.

Mohnish: captivator, one who enamours.

Mokshit: liberated.

Monal: bird.

Monish: lord of mind.

Morley: moor.

Moti: pearl.

Mridant: passing through a constellation.

Mridugir: soft-voiced.

Mridur: water-born.

Mrigalochan: one with eyes like that of a deer.

Mrigānk: spotted like dear, wind, moon, camphor.

Mrigankmouli: one with moon in his hair (i.e. Lord Shiva).

Mrigankshekhar: one with moon on his head (i.e.Lord Shiva).

Mrigendra: lion.

Mrigesh: lion.

Mrinal: lotus root, lotus fibre.

Mrinank: moon.

Mrinendra: lion.

Mritunjay: overcoming death, Shiva.

Muchir: generous, virtuous, wind.

Muchukund: cloud.

Mudgal: always happy, enchanting, hammer.

Mudir: cloud.

Mudit: happy, joyous, gay.

Mudra: joyous, happy.

Mugdhendu: lovely moon, new moon.

Muhammed: praised One.

Mukesh: lord of freedom, Shiva.

Mukta: freed, opened, pearl, emancipated, delivered.

Muktanand: happiness of freedom.

Muktesh: lord of freedom.

Mukul: bud, body, soul, hidden, covered.

Mukund: liberator, precious stone, Vishnu, Krishna.

Mukur: bud, mirror, double jasmine.

Mukuṭ: crown, diadem, crest.

Mukula: the bud.

Mukulita: full of blossom.

Mukunda: a precious stone.

Mukura: a bud.

Mulka: country.

Mura: a name of the demon.

Murita: slaved, bound.

Muru: detached.

Muneesh: chief of ascetics.

Munivar: best among ascetics.

Murād: desire, wish.

Murali: a flute.

Muralidhar: one holding a flute (i.e. Lord Krishna).

Murāri: lotus root, Krishna.

Murray: sailor.

Mushand: strong, powerful.

Musheera: the advice.

Muheera: Lord Kāma.

Mukhara: talkative.

Mudra: happy.

Mukteesha: supreme liberation.

Musalin: armed with club.

Meda: a name of the herb.

Mehuta: rain

N

Naagdhar: one who wears cobra (Lord Shiva).

Naagpal, Nagpal: saviour of serpents (the cobras).

Naagpati: king of serpents (Vaasuki).

Naagraj: king of serpents, Sheshnaag.

Nabha: expanding the sky, atmosphere, Shiva.

Nābhāg: moving in the sky, bird.

Nabhas: clouds, mist, sun, sky, vapour, rainy season.

Nabhit: bold, fearless.

Nabhod: sky-risen cloud.

Nabhoj: born in sky.

Nabhomani: jewel of the sky (sun).

Nabhya: central, Shiva.

Nachiketa: fire.

Nadal: fortunate.

Nadeen: lord of rivers.

Nadeesh: god of river (ocean).

Nadiesh: ocean.

Nadin: ocean.

Nagaj: mountain-born.

Nagdhar: one who adornes mountain (Lord Krishna).

Nagendra: mountain lord.

Nagendra: lord of mountains (Himalaya).

Nagesh: lord of mountains, Shiva.

Nāgesh: lord of serpents, lord of elephants, noble elephant.

Nahush: fellowman, Vishnu, Krishna.

Naimish: momentary, transient.

Naināar: observer, preceptor.

Nākesh: Indra, lord of the sky.

Nakhraj: moon.

Nakshatresh: moon, camphor.

Nakuja: born of an anthill.

Nakul: son, musical instrument.

Nakulesh: Shiva.

Nāleek: arrow, spear, lotus, limb.

Nalesh: king of flowers.

Nalik: arrow, spear, lotus flower.

Nalin: lotus, water, lily, crane, indigo plant, water.

Nalinaksh: lotus-eyed.

Nalinesh: Brahma.

Nalinikant: husband of lotus (sun).

Nalund : nectar of flower.

Nāman: name, renowned, form, mark.

Naman: lowing, offering, homage.

Namasit: revered, auspicious, sacred, virtuous.

Namat: bending, bowing.

Namdev: poet, saint.

Namesh: lord of obeisance, divine being, worshipped.

Nāmgiri: sacred mountain.

Nāmi: of great fame, Vishnu.

Namit: bowed, worshipper, devotee, modest, humble.

Nāmuvar: famed.

Namya: worthy of obeisance, venerable.

Nānak: without darkness, happy, griefless, fearless, coin, a Sikh guru.

Nanda: joy, happiness, delight, Vishnu.

Nandak: delighting, rejoicing, gladdening.

Nandakishor: wiz-kid, Lord Krishna.

Nandakumar: lord Krishna.

Nandan: rejoicing, gladdening.

Nandant: rejoicing, gladdening, son, king, friend.

Nandapal: lord Krishna.

Nandeesh: lord of pleasure, lord of bulls, Shiva.

Nandi: one who pleases others, the divine bull.

Nandik: pleasure giving.

Nandikānt: ocean.

Nandil: delighted, pleased.

Nandin: son, happy, Shiva's bull, Shiva.

Nandish: lord Shiva (Nandishwar).

N antra: praise, enlogy, Shiva.

Napāt: descendant, offspring, son, path of the gods.

Naradev: god of men.

Naran: belonging to men, that which is human.

Nārang: orange-hued, human form, living being, twin, orange tree.

Narayana: lord Vishnu, refuge of man, god.

Nardan: roarer, praising aloud, celebrating.

Narendra: lord of men.

Narendranath: king of kings, emperor.

Naresh: king of men.

Narhari: man-lion (Nara simha).

Narmad: bringing delight.

Narman: humour, joke, wit, play, jest, sport.

Narottam: best amongst men, Lord Vishnu.

Narpāl: king.

Narsimha: half lion & half man.

Nartan: dance.

Narun̄: leader of men.

Nāsheer: leading, ahead, atop.

Nassir: protector.

Natesh: lord of dancers, Shiva.

Nateshwar: god of drama (Lord Shiva).

Nāthan: controller, protector, Krishna.

Natraj: king among actors, lord Shiva.

Naunihāl: new crop, child.

Navaj: new born, new moon.

Navajyot: new light, first light of day.

Naval: new, novel.

Navan: act of praising, eulogy.

Navaneet: new butter, mild, gentle, soft, Krishna.

Navasar: pearl ornament.

Navatej: new energy.

Naveen: new, novel.

Navendu: new moon (the moon a night after amavasya).

Navinchandra: same as Navendu.

Navodit: newly risen, newborn, sun.

Navrang: beautiful.

Navratan: nine jewels.

Nawalkishor: lord Krishna.

Nāyak: leader, lord, principal, main gem of a necklace.

Nayan: leading, directing, eye.

Nayanadeep: light of the eye.

Nayat: leading, guiding.

Neehār: mist, fog, dew.

Neekāsh: appearance, look.

Neel: blue.

Neelābh: of bluish colour, moon.

Neelād: bestower of blue, giver of water, cloud.

Neelādri: blue peak.

Neelaj: produced in blue mountain.

Neelāksh: blue-eyed.

Neelam: emerald.

Neelamani: blue jewel.

Neelambar: blue-cloth, blue sky.

Neelambuj: blue lotus.

Neelgreev: lord Shiva.

Neelkamal: blue lotus.

Neelkant: a jewel, Lord Vishnu.

Neelkanth: one with blue neck (e.g. the bird peacock, Lord Shiva).

Neemāy: adjusted, ascetic.

Neerad: water-giver, cloud.

Neerāj: illuminate, irradiate.

Neerājan: offering of light to deity.

Neerat: engrossed, absorbed, happy.

Neerav: free from sound, silent still, quiet.

Neerūp: formless, ether, air, wind, a gold.

Neet: leader.

Neeti: policy, conduct, guidance, moral conduct, management, prudence.

Neetil: bearer of moral code, forehead.

Neetin: having knowledge of law, policy-maker, moralist.

Nelson: son of a champion.

Nemi: edge, rim, thunderbolt.

Nevin: worshipper, nephew.

Nibodh: knowledge.

Nidarshin: seeing, pleasing, familiar.

Nidhān: treasure house.

Nidhip: lord of treasure.

Nidhish: lord of treasure (Kuber).

Nidhruv: constant, faithful, perserving.

Nidosh: faultless, innocent.

Nihāl: contented, happy.

Nihar: mist, dew, fog.

Nikāma: pleasure, desire, wish.

Nikash: touchstone.

Nikāsh: horizon.

Niketan: house, abode.

Nikhil: complete, total, all, entire.

Nikhilesh: lord of the universe.

Nikunj: abode, bush, abode of love, beautiful, enchanting, mysterious.

Nilay: home, abode.

Nilaj: blue steel, produced in the blue mountain.

Nilāksh: blue-eyed.

Nilay: place of refuge.

Nilesh, Neelesh: blue God (Lord Krishna), god of blue sky (i.e. moon).

Nilibh: moon, with a blue colour, bee, cloud.

Nimal: spotless, pure, clean, bright.

Nimaloch: setting sun.

Niman: healthy, excellent.

Nimay: adjusted.

Nimesh: moment, eye-wink.

Nimey: to be measured.

Nimish: twinkling of an eye.

Nimit: fixed. rooted, raised, erected.

Ninād: gentle murmur, hum, sound.

Ninādit: resonant, full of sound.

Nipāk: intelligent, wise, chief.

Nipun̄: adept, skilful, adroit, clever, efficient, complete, perfect, sharp, kind.

Nirad: given by water, cloud.

Nirāg: free from passion.

Niraj: born from water (eg lotus flower, pearl).

Nirajit: lighted.

Nirālā: unique.

Niramesh: pure vegetarian.

Niramitra: son of pandava Sahadeva.

Niranjan: without a black spot, spotless, pure, passionless, unpainted.

Nirankar: with no shape (God).

Nirāntak: free from all that brings end, fearless, Shiva.

Nirantar: without a gap, perpetual.

Niras: without anger.

Nirat: engrossed, pleased, absorbed.

Nirav: without sound, silent.

Nirbhay: fearless.

Nirdhar: one who holds water (cloud).

Nirek: without anger.

Nirguṇ: without attributes.

Niring: still, not flickering, immovable.

Nirijar: young, fresh, immortal, gold, ambrosia.

Nirish: free, without any owner.

Nirjanesh: Shiva.

Nirjay: complete victory, conquest.

Nirjit: won, conquered.

Nirlep: unstained, unsmeared, Shiva.

Nirmad: without intoxication, sobre, humble, modest, quiet.

Nirmal: clean, spotless, pure, sinless, bright, shining.

Nirmam: unselfish, Shiva.

Nirmantu: faultless, innocent.

Nirmanyu: angerless.

Nirmay: healthy.

Nirmit: created, built, fashioned.

Nirmol: priceless, rare.

Nirosh: without anger.

Niruj: healthy, robust.

Nirupam: unequalled, unparalleled, unique.

Nirval: sacred, pious.

Nirvar: unique, without a superior, excellent.

Nirvāt: sheltered, calm.

Nirvikār: unchangeable.

Nirvishank: fearless, doubtless.

Nirvrit: happy, peaceful, contented.

Nishad: the 7th note on Indian musical scale, one who eats only in the night.

Nishādish: moon.

Nishākānt: beloved of night, moon.

Nishākar: maker of night, moon.

Nishang: moving freely, unattached, unselfish.

Nishank: fearless, free from risk.

Nishankar: creator of night, moon.

Nishānt: closing night, daybreak, tranquil, quiet.

Nishar: warm cloth.

Nishaṭh: honest.

Nishchal: unmovable, unshakable.

Nisheeman: grand, infinite, unbounded.

Nishesh: god of night (moon).

Nishinath: lord of night (moon) (Nishipati, Nishipal).

Nishith: born of night, midnight.

Nishok: one without sorrow, happy.

Nisidh: gift, offering.

Nisit: eager, excited, iron, steel, prepared, sharp.

Nistul: unequalled.

Nistush: pure.

Nitaran: first light of dawn.

Niteesh: the God of law, one well versed in law.

Nitin: follower of right path.

Nitish: lord of correct path.

Nityānand: eternal happiness.

Nityasundar: ever good-looking.

Nityayaj: never distracted.

Nivan: reigned, tied.

Nivāt: safe, unhurt, secure, compact, wind-sheltered.

Nivedan: offering, announcement, dedication.

Niveet: adorned with.

Nivid: instructions, invocation.

Nivrutti: separation from world.

Nāgāri: enemy of serpent.

Nāgantaka: one who destroys serpent.

Nāgesha: king of the serpents.

Nāgeshwara: Lord of the snakes.

Nāksha: to attain.

Nālika: lotus, arrow.

Nāman: well known, famed.

Nāsatya: helpful.

Niyam: control, determine, fasten, govern, grant, restrain.

Norman: man from the north.

Nripanjay: conqueror of men.

Nripendra: the king of kings.

Nūri: fire.

Nabhas: sky, clouds, mistry.

Nrriga: originated from man.

Nrrgavara: best among man.

Nrripa: king.

Nrripamana: saluted by man.

Nrrit: sacred thread worn round the neck.

Nrritu: dancing.

Nyāyavid: one who knows law.

O

Oakes: from the oak-tree grove.

Obalesh: lord of linga, Shiva.

Oberon: noble, elf, bear.

Odan: food, cloud, boiled rice.

Oḍie: melody.

Oḍongo: second of twins.

Ogañ: wave, united, assembled.

Ogḍen: from the oak valley.

Ohas: thought, appreciation, mode of conveyance.

Ojal: vision, splendour.

Ojas: energy, power, splendour, strength, viriḷity, water, appearance, light.

Ojaseen: strong, powerful.

Ojaski: courageous, shining.

Ojasvi: vigorous, powerful.

Ojasya: mighty, strong, virulent.

Olaf: ancestor's descendant.

Oliver: olive tree.

Oliyā: holy man.

Omā: commander.

Omair: problem solver.

Oman: life-giving, protection, friend, favour.

Omananḍ: joy of Om.

Omar: gifted speaker, famous, first son, disciple, long life.

Omesh: lord of the syllable Om.

Omiḍ: hope.

Omkār: syllable Om.

Omkresh: Shiva.

Omkarnath: Shiva.

Omprakāsh: light from Om, sacred light, light spread by Om.

Omrān: solid structure.

Omswarup: like Om.

Oneal: torchlight.

Oojam: enthusiasm.

Oorjit: powerful, strong.

Opash: support, pillar.

Orā: prayer.

Orbo: privileged.

Orie: gold.

Orion: son of fire.

Orlanḍo: land of gold.

Orson: spearman's son, bear.

Osmond: Godly protector, red.

Obal: the Shivalinga.

Obbana: Lord Shiva.

Oblesha: Lord Shiva.

Odana: cloud.

Ogān: wave.

Ogana: assembled.

Osāma: like a lion.

Osborn: divine, bear.

Oscar: deer, lover.

Oshadish: moon, camphor.

Oswalḍ: divinely powerful.

Otar: incarnation of God.

Othello: prosperous.

Oṭto: wealthy.

Oviḍ: sheep.

Owen: yew tree.

Ojasvin: energetic.

Ojisthā: strongest.

Ojodā: giver of strength.

Omrao: king.

Oni: protection.

Ooti: protection.

P

Packārḍ: one who packs.

Padāti: pedestrian, foot soldier.

Padamdeesh: Vishnu.

Padmabandhu: friend of lotus (bee , sun).

Padmádhar: one who holds a lotus (Lord Vishnu).

Padmahāsan: lotus-like smile, Vishnu.

Padmaj: lotus-born, Brahma.

Padmakant: husband of lotus (sun).

Padmakar: jewel, lord Vishnu, lake with lotuses.

Padmalochan: lotus eyed.

Padmanabh: one with lotus in his navel (Lord Vishnu).

Padmapani: lord Bramha.

Padmesh: lord of lotus, Brahma, Vishnu.

Pameshay: sleeping in lotus, Vishnu.

Padmin: lotus-like, lotus plucker, lotus-lover, elephant.

Padmineesh: lord of lotuses.

Padvāy: leader, guide.

Pājas: firmness, glitter, brightness, sheen, vigour, strength.

Pakshil: full of feathers, full of examples, full of logic.

Paksheendra: king of birds.

Pakshman: eyelashes, leaf, wing, flower sepal.

Pālak: protector, prince, sovereign.

Palaksha: white.

Palāsh: leaf, petal, foliage, green.

Pālin: protecting, keeping, guarding.

Pālit: grey, aged, mouse.

Pallav: bud, blossom, shoot, spray, sprout.

Panas: tree dweller, monkey.

Pan̄av: small drum, cymbal.

Pānchāl: Shiva.

Pancham: clever, beautiful.

Panduranga: one with a pale white complexion.

Panik: hand.

Pāṅini: with beautiful hands, skilled.

Panit: admired, praised.

Pankaj: mud-born, lotus.

Pankajeet: eagle (Garuda).

Pannalal: a jewel.

Parāg: flower pollen, fragrant, fame, celebrity, poder.

Pāragat: one who has safely crossed over, pure, holy.

Pāraj: gold.

Pārak: carrying over, delivering, pleasing, saving, satisfying.

Paramak: best, greatest, highest.

Paramānand: eternal bliss.

Paramār: beyond death.

Paramartha: highest or divine truth.

Paramesh: Supreme Lord, Vishnu, Supreme Being.

Paramit: measured, regulated.

Paramjeet: highest success.

Paran: leaf, feather.

Parantap: conquerrer.

Paras: a stone (mythical stone) which can turn anything into gold.

Parāsh: iron.

Parāshar: crusher, destroyer.

Paraspā: protector.

Parāyush: attaining highest age.

Pareemaṅ: bounty, plenty, quality.

Parees: touch stone.

Paresh: highest lord, Brahma.

Parighosh: loud sound.

Pārijāt: born, coral jasmine.

Parijeet: famous, illustrious.

Pariket: against desire.

Parijman: surrounding, fire, moon, omnipresent.

Parijwal: shining brightly.

Parikshit: tested, fully perceived, aode, extending, surrounding, heaven and earth.

Parimal: fragrance, perfume.

Parimān: abundant, plenty.

Parindan: gift, present.

Parindra: lion.

Parinut: praised, acclaimed.

Paripreet: full of love and affection.

Paritosh; delight.

Parjanya: cloud, rain.

Parjat: coral tree with fragrant flowers.

Pārker: cultivated land.

Parña: leaf, full of leaves, surrounded by leaves, feather, surrounded by feathers.

Parnād: feeding on leaves.

Paroksh: beyond observation.

Parry: son of Harry.

Pārshad: companion, associate, spectator.

Pārtha: son of earth, prince, king.

Parthasarathi: charioteer of Partha (Lord Krishna).

Pārthiv: of the earth, earthen, royal, king, prince, warrior.

Paru: limb, member, paradise, sky, ocean, mountain.

Pāru: fire, sun.

Parush: sharp, keen, arrow, violent.

Parvatesh: mountain king.

Parvateshwar: god of mountains (Himalaya).

Parvatinandan: son of Parvati (Ganesh / Kartikeya).

Parvit: surrounded, covered, encompassed, veiled.

Pārshak: foot ornament.

Paryānk: bed, sitting posture.

Pashunath: lord of animals (lord Shiva, lion).

Pashupati: animal farmer, Lord Shiva.

Pashyat: visible, conspicuous.

Pātangi: son of sun.

Patanjali: one to be worshipped.

Paṭav: clever, dextrous, sharp.

Pāthas: air, place, spot, water.

Pāthya: heavenly.

Paṭu: clever, keen, intense, sharp, skilful, strong.

Paṭul: yellow.

Pāvak: purifier, pure, clear, fire, bright, shining.

Pāvaki: son of fire, Vishnu.

Pavamān: purified, clear flowing, wind.

Pavan: breeze, air, wind.

Pāvan: purifying, sacred, fire, incense.

Pavankumar: Bhim, Hanuman (son of the wind).

Pavansut, Pavanputra: son of wind (Bhim, Hanuman).

Pāvant: purity, sanctity, holiness.

Pavitar: pure, holy.

Payas: milk, juice, rain, water, power.

Payod: milk-giving, water-giving.

Payoj: lotus.

Pāyu: guard, protector.

Pehaj: first-born.

Perry: pear tree.

Perth: thorny bush.

Peru: drinking, swelling, rescuing, fire, ocean, sun.

Peshal: adorned, beautiful, charming, decorated, soft, tender, Vishnu.

Phalgun: a month from our Hindu Calender.

Phanibhushan: one who wears a snake (Lord Shiva).

Phaninath: lord of serpents (Sheshnag, Vasuki).

Phanindra: king of Gods (Sheshnag, Vasuki).

Phanindranath: lord Vishnu.

Phoolendu: the full moon.

Pierce: rock.

Pinak: bow of Shiva.

Pitambar: yellow cloth, lord Vishnu.

Pitvas: Krishna.

Piyal: large tree.

Piyush: nectar.

Poshit: nourished, cherished, guarded.

Prabhākar: creator of light, Shiva, sun, moon.

Prabhān: light, radiance, splendour.

Prabhanjan: dust storm.

Prabhas: brilliance, light.

Prabhāsan: illuminating.

Prabhāt: dawn, sunrise, morning.

Prabhāv: cause of existence, beauty, dignity, majesty, origin, might, power, strength, splendour, creation, lord Shiva.

Prabhu: creator, abundant, eternal, god, king, lord, mighty, powerful, God.

Prabir: hero, brave one (Praveer).

Prabodh: awakening, consciousness, knowledge, understanding.

Prabodhan: knowledge.

Prabuddha: knowledgeable.

Prachetas: with an awakened mind, wise, happy, conscious, delighted, clever.

Pradarsh: appearance, order.

Pradatta: bestowed, given.

Pradeep; light, radiance.

Pradhyot: ray of light.

Pradnesh: lord of wisdom.

Pradosh: sunset, evening.

Pradyut: lighted, to begin shining.

Prafulla: pleasant, cheerful, in full bloom.

Praful: happy.

Prāgahi: holder of knowledge.

Pragat: well-sung, reciting, highly praised, lyric, song.

Pragitya: famous, illustrious.

Prāgra: highest point, apex, summit.

Pragun: efficient, full of qualities, honest, right, straight.

Prahās: laughter, display, coloured-splendour, appearance, Shiva.

Prahlād: delight, happiness, joy.

Prajānin: efficient.

Prajapati: king, Bramha.

Prajas: born, produced, bring forth.

Prajāti: generation, production, delivery.

Prajesh: king, Rohini Constallation, lord Brahma.

Prajin: swift, moving, air, wind.

Prajit: conquering, overpowering.

Prajivin: active, energetic, bubbling with life.

Prajnay: Rama, Indra.

Prakām: intense yearning, desire, delight, fulfilment, joy.

Prākar: doing well, friendship, respect.

Prakāsh: appearance, fame, glory, brightness, dearness, light, lustre, splendour, sunshine, visible, renown.

Praket: perception, appearance, intelligence, knowledge.

Prākrit: nature, original.

Prakul: handsome body.

Pramad: delight, joy, pleasure.

Pramahas: of great splendour.

Pramat: wise, prudent.

Pramath: horse.

Pramesh: master of accurate knowledge.

Pramit: moderate, limited, measured out.

Pramod: delight, pleasure, joy, happiness.

Prān: life.

Pranad: loud sound, reverberation.

Pranal: waterway.

Pranav: mystical syllable Om.

Prānavesh: Shiva.

Pranay: leader, guide, conductor, love, affection.

Prāndhan: a dear person.

Praneet: a river.

Praneet: agreeable, pleasing.

Prānesh: lord of life, lord of breath.

Pranet: leader.

Praney: obedient.

Prānjal: honest, upright, sincere.

Prannath: lord of life (most beloved person), husband.

Pranod: directing, driving, leading.

Prānshu: tall, high, long, strong, intense.

Pranut: celebrated, extolled, praised.

Prārochan: excitement.

Prasād: blessing, gift, boon.

Prasadhan: to please, to gratify.

Prasal: cool, tranquil.

Prasandhi: expert negotiator, peacemaker.

Prasang: adherence, devotion, attachment, context, connection, union.

Prasanna: pleased, bright, clear, distinct, placid, pure, tranquil, trade, soothed, cheerful.

Prasata: father of Draupad.

Prasena: with an expert army.

Prasham: calm, cool, reposed, peaceful, healing, autumn.

Prashan: winner, successful.

Prashānt: calm, quiet.

Prashin: Krishna.

Prasoon: flower.

Prastav: hymn of praise, chant, song.

Prastha: expanse, plain.

Prāsthu: very quick, speedy.

Prasun: blssom, flower.

Prasvār: sacred syllable Om.

Pratān: shoot, tendril, branching out.

Pratāp: brilliance, glory, heat, energy, majesty, power, strength, splendour, warmth.

Prātar: glorious, shining.

Prateek: look, appearance, image, symbol, part, member, limb.

Prateep: opposite.

Prateer: shore, bank.

Prateet: know, appeared, manifest, recognised, wise.

Prathit: extended, spreed, known, celebrated, Vishnu.

Pratibh: resplendent.

Pratinav: new, young.

Prativesh: Shiva.

Pratosh: extreme delight.

Pratush: delighted, to delight in.

Pratyush: every morning, dawn.

Pravan: conquer, vanquish.

Pravar: chief, best, eminent, excellent, eldest, principal.

Pravarjay: renunciation.

Pravasu: wealthy.

Praveen: skilful, adroit, clever.

Praveer: excelling heroes, chief, prince.

Pravek: excellent, chief, principal.

Pravitra: protector, friend, patron.

Prayag: confluence of Ganga-Jamuna-Saraswati.

Prayas: delight, enjoyment, pleasure.

Prayuj: motive, impulse.

Prayut: mixed with, mingled with, conjoined with.

Preet: pleased, delighted, joyous, happy.

Preetam: beloved, husband.

Preetidutt: gifted with love.

Preetimān: kind, affectionate.

Preetish: God of love.

Preetiwardhan: one who increases love.

Prem: love, affection.

Premal: full of love.

Preman: love, affection, favour, kindness.

Premanand: joy of love.

Prescott: residence.

Prayadarshi: one who is liked by all.

Priank: pleased, satisfied.

Prinit: happy, contented.

Prishad: spotted, antelope, tiger.

Pritam: lover.

Prithu: broad, spacious.

Prithvijaj: king of the earth.

Priyadarshan: beautiful, good-looking.

Priyak: loving, bee, deer.

Priyanvad: sweet talking person.

Priyaranjan: beloved.

Priteesh: lord of the world.

Prithi: of earth, material, large.

Prithvi: earth.

Pudgal: beautiful, handsome, living, body, ego, soul, Shiva.

Pukhraj: a yellow jewel.

Pulak: thrill of joy, gem.

Puloman: thrilled in ecstasy.

Punān: bright, clear, purified.

Pundarik: lotus.

Puneesh: lord of the pious.

Puneet: holy, sacred, pious, purified, cleaned.

Pūran: ocean.

Purandar: lord Indra, lord Vishnu.

Puranjan: life, soul.

Puranjay: conqueror of city.

Purendra: Vishnu.

Purjeet: Shiva.

Pūrṇa: complete, entire, abundant, auspicious, content, full, capable. strong, wealthy.

Pūrnendu: full moon.

Purochan: builder of city.

Purū: many much, abundant, every, heaven, paradise, flower pollen.

Puruday: full of compassion.

Purujit: conqueror of city.

Purumitra: friend of city.

Purushottam: best amongst men, lord Rama.

Pūshan: nourishes, protector.

Pushkal: abundant, best, complete, copious, full, excellent, loud, magnificent, powerful, purified, Shiva.

Pushkar: blue lotus, arrow, heaven, sky, sun, sword blade, Krishna, Shiva.

Pushpad: who gives flowers.

Pushpaj: flower-born, nectar.

Pushpak: Kubers plane taken away by Ravan.

Pushpakar: the Spring season (Vasant), flower season.

Pushpaketu: Kamdev, cupid.

Pushpam: topaz-eyed, eyes brilliant like topaz, flower.

Pushpavān: possessing flowers, flowering, fragrant.

Pushpendra: lord of flowers.

Pushpesh: lord of flowers.

Pushpit: flowered, having flowers, blooming.

Praveka: excellent, chief.

Preena: satisfied.

Pulaha: creator of creature.

Pulaka: a thrill of excitement.

Pulakeshin: extremely happy.

Pullina: a bank of river.

Puloman: a thrill in rapture.

Pundareeka: lotus flower.

Pushya: nourishment, blossom, best of anything.

Pyarelal: lord Krishna.

Puneesha: sacred.

Puradvisha: enemy of city.

Purahan: one who killed Pura.

Puranjana: Lord Varuna.

Puruja: bord of Puru.

Pushpam: topaz eyed.

Puttala: pure.

Pushpin: blooming.

Q

Qābil: efficient, skilful, able.

Qādim: old, primitive, ancient.

Qādir: brave, conqueror, powerful.

Qāhir: courageous, brave, destroyer, conqueror, Mars.

Qālān: handsome, noble.

Qāmār: moon.

Qāsim: divider.

Qātar: crown, blessed.

Qayyām: God, immortal.

Qayyim: just, strong, Quran.

Qudāmāh: courage.

Qudrat: power, strength, potency, nature.

Quennel: oak tree.

Quin: strong.

R

Rabhas: shining, impetuous, zeal, fierce, strong, wild, passion.

Rachit: produceed, prepared, fashioned.

Raḍcliff: red cliff.

Rāddhi: perfection, completion, accomplishment, success.

Rādesh: lord of Radha, Krishna.

Radhakrishna: Radha & Lord Krishna.

Radheya: son of Radha .i e Karna.

Rafat: ascending.

Rāghav: Raghu descendant, Rama.

Raghu: fleet, rapid, light.

Raghukar: inspirer, accelerator.

Raghukumār: son of Raghu.

Raghuveer/vir: brave man of the Raghu clan (Rama).

Rāgi: full of love, affectionate, coloured, delighting.

Rāhul: able, efficient.

Raivat: wealthy.

Raj: king.

Rājadeep: lamp of kings, lamp among kings.

Rājahans: royal swan, excellent, king.

Rājak: illuminating, splendid, prince, king.

Rājan: king, ruler, moon.

Rajendra: emperor, king of kings.

Rajesh: god of kings, emperor.

Rajiv: lotus flower.

Rajkumar: prince.

Rājneel: royal blue, emerald.

Rajaneesh: lord of night, moon.

Rajanikānt: beloved of the night, moon.

Rajanikar: night maker, moon.

Rajas: silvery, autumn, dust, mist, passion, pollen, vapour.

Rajat: silver, ivory, mind, bright, pleasant, pearl bright.

Rajawant: with kingly qualities.

Rajatādri: silver mountain.

Rajeev: streaked, striped, deer, elephant, blue lotus.

Rajit: bright, brilliant, illuminant.

Rākā: full-moon day.

Rākāneesh: lord of night, full moon.

Rākesh: lord of full moon, Shiva.

Rakhan: protect, save.

Raktakamal: a red lotus.

Raktānk: red-marked, coral.

Ralph: wolf, wise counsel.

Rāma: enchanting, all-pervading, omnipresent, causing rest, charming, delight, dark, delight, lovely, pleasant, Vishnu.

Rāmak: sporting, dallying, delighting, gratifying, lover, sporting.

Ramākānt: beloved of Rama, Vishnu.

Rāmakinkar: servant of Rama.

Ramakrishna: Rama & Krishna.

Rāmakrit: causing rest.

Rāmal: lover.

Raman: pleasing, beloved, Kamdev.

Ramaṇ: charming, delightful, pleasing, lover, husband.

Ramaṇik: attractive, pleasing, worth loving.

Rāmānij: younger brother of Rama, Krishna.

Ramanuja: born after Lord Rama i.e. Lakshman.

Rāmasetu: the bridge of Rama.

Ramati: lover, time, paradise.

Ramdas: devotee (a servant) of Rama, Hanuman.

Ramendra: lord of Rama, Vishnu.

Ramesh: lord of Rama, Vishnu.

Rāmee: right, proper.

Rāmil: lover.

Ramit: delighted, gladdened, loved.

Ramra: beauty, splendour.

Ramsey: ram's land.

Ramyashree: most desired, Vishnu.

Rāna: joy, joy of battle, delight, pleasure, battle, sound, motherly love.

Ranadheer: patient in battle, patient warrior.

Ranādya: beginning of sound, start of battle.

Ranak: warrior, king.

Rananjay: victor in war.

Ranesh: lord of battle, Shiva.

Ranga: colour, amusement, arena, battlefield, colour, love, music.

Rangan: dancing, loving, merry-making.

Ranganath: lord Vishnu.

Rangesh: hero of a play.

Rangit: well-coloured, handsome.

Ranjan: colouring, contenting, delighting, entertaining pleasing.

Ranjit: victorious in battle, happy, delighted.

Ranjul: charming, handsome, bestower of entertainment.

Ransee: cheerful, delightful.

Rantinār: warrior.

Ranveer: warrior, hero of the battle.

Ranvit: gay, joyous, lovely, pleasant.

Rasesh: lord of sentiments.

Raseshwar: quick-silver.

Rasheem: beam, ray.

Rāshi: aesthetic, elegant, passionate, sentimental, with discrimination.

Rashul: passionate, beautiful, delighting, elegant, discriminating, graceful, humorous, tasteful.

Rashmin: bearer of rays, sun, moon.

Rasik: admirer, lover.

Rasraj: king of liquids (mercury -element), romance (Shringar ras).

Rasvant: affectionate.

Ratan: gem.

Rateesh: god of Ratee, husband of Ratee (Kamdev).

Ratharvi: moving like a chariot.

Rathik: rider of a chariot.

Rathin: mover on chariot.

Rathindra: lord of chariot.

Ratik: delighted, joyful, loved, satisfied.

Rativant: beautiful, fascinating.

Ratnadeep: jewelled lamp, illuminating jewel.

Ratnākar: jewel mine.

Ratnam: jewel, precious object.

Ratnāng: coral.

Ratnānk: Vishnu's vehicle.

Ratnapār: beyond jewels.

Ratnarāj: king of jewels, ruby.

Ratnāchis: shining like jewel.

Ratnesh: lord of jewels.

Ratnin: possessing jewels, receiving gifts.

Ratnottam: best jewel.

Ratopal: red lotus.

Rātrij: born at night, star.

Ratujit: conqueror of truth.

Rātul: seeking truth, desiring, interested.

Raubhya: misty, foggy.

Ravath: humming, calling out, Indian cuckoo.

Raveesh: fashion, mode.

Ravi: sun.

Ravidās: devotee of sun.

Ravidev: lord of sun.

Ravideepta: lit by sun.

Ravij: born of sun.

Ravikānt: beloved of sun, sunstone.

Ravikiran: sunray.

Ravikeerti: with fame as bright as sun, famed.

Ravilochan: sun-bright eyes, fiery-eyed, Shiva.

Ravinandan: son of sun.

Ravināth: whose lord is sun, lotus.

Ravindra: lord of sun, sun and Indra conjoined.

Ravindranath: lord Vishnu.

Ravinshu: Kamdev (Cupid).

Ravirāj: king of sun.

Ravirath: chariot of sun.

Ravish: sun-desirer.

Ravishankar: lord of sun.

Ravishekhar: one whose crest is sun, sun-crested.

Ravisuta: son of sun.

Rāyāṇa: ever-moving, forceful.

Rayidā: bestowing wealth.

Razāk: devotee.

Rebha: singer of praise.

Reeve: bailiff.

Remingṭon: from the raven's home.

Renesh: lord of love.

Reṇumat: sandy.

Reshman: storm, whirlwind.

Reuben: behold a son.

Revat: wealthy, beautiful, brilliant, prosperous, splendid.

Ribhav: skilled, glowing sunrays.

Ribhuksh: most prudent.

Ribhvan: clever, skilful, wise.

Richak: desire, hymn-effected, wish.

Richarḍ: powerful ruler, brave.

Richeek: knower of hymns, praiser.

Riddhimān: prosperous, successful.

Rigmin: jubilant with praise.

Rijul: simple, innocent, honest.

Rijut: honesty, simplicity.

Riksh: the best, excellent, ape, bear.

Riksharāj: lord of stars, lord of apes, lord of bears.

Rikta: of true, nature, simple, honest, truthful.

Rikthan: gold, heir.

Rimā: freed, emancipated, released.

Rimon: pomegranate.

Ripudaman: one who defeats his enemies.

Ripunjay: vanquisher of foes.

Rishabh: bull, most excellent.

Rishi: chanter of sacred hymns, seer, sage, author of *Vedic* hymns, halo.

Rishik: belonging to seers.

Rishirāj: lord of sages.

Rishul: sunrays, glowing fire, great, powerful, wise, firebrand.

Rishvanjas: with sublime power.

Ritadhām: house of truth, ray of light, Krishna.

Ritajit: gaining truth.

Ritam: like truth, fixed, settled, divine, sacred action, duty, right.

Ritap: guarding during truth.

Ritav: of a season.

Ritesh: lord of truth.,

Riteeshā: subduing enemies.

Ritoday: true speech.

Ritujeet, Rutujit: conquerer of seasons.

Ritunāth: lord of seasons.

Ritunjay: conqueror of seasons, conqueror of truth.

Riturāj: lord of seasons.

Ritva: belonging to seasons.

Ritvik: sacrificing at the appropriate time, present.

Rityu: truthful.

Rizvān: practice.

Robbil: bright in fame.

Robbin: renowned, illustrious.

Robeṛt: bright.

Rocha: enlightens, shining, radiant.

Rochak: tasteful, enlightening, brightening, agreeable.

Rochamān: shining, bright.

Rochan: agreeable, charming, pleasing, shining, radiant.

Rochiras: aura, glow, light.

Rochishnat: possessing, light.

Rochit: glorious, delightful.

Rodas: heaven and earth.

Roḍney: famous.

Rohak: rising, ascending.

Rohan̄: ascending, rising, climbing, blossom, Vishnu.

Rohant: ascending, tree.

Rohil: ascended, risen.

Rohin̄: ascending, rising, banyan tree, sandalwood tree, Vishnu.

Rohineesh: lord of Rohini (Krishna's wife), moon.

Rohit: fed, sun, precious stone-studded ornament, blood, rainbow, saffron.

Rohitak: red-hued.

Rohitashwa: one with red horse, fire.

Rola: painting.

Roladev: lord of painting.

Roman: pledge.

Romik: magnet, salt.

Romir: interesting, pleasant.

Roop: form, beauty, image.

Roshan: radiant, passionate, touchstone, silverstone.

Rowan: red-haired.

Ruchak: golden, agreeable, large, ornamental, fortune-bringer, sweet-voiced, dove.

Rucheru: beautiful, charming, pleasing.

Rucheju: shining, delightful.

Ruchikar: causing desire.

Ruchir: beautiful, bright, brilliant, agreeable, golden, radiant, splendid, handsome, shining, saffron plant.

Ruchit: delighted, sweet, dainty, bright, shining, pleasant.

Ruchya: bright, beautiful, desirable, pleasant, radiant, lover.

Rudhikrā: rising, famous, ascending.

Rudhir: red, blood, Mars.

Rudra: angry, lord Shiva.

Ruḍyarḍ: from the red gate.

Ruhan̄i: of higher values, spiritual.

Rujul: simple, honest.

Rukma: radiant, gold, ornament, sun.

Rukmādhar: possessing gold.

Rukmat: bright, shining.

Rukmeshu: golden-arrowed.

Rukmin: wearing golden ornaments.

Ruman: a friend of Sugriva.

Rumra: beautiful, tawny.

Rūpak: form, figure, sign.

Rūpal: made of silver.

Rūpam: beauty, form.

Rūpang: with a beautiful body.

Rūpāshray: receptable of beauty.

Rritu: season, fixed time.

Rrivan: happy with praise.

Rucheru: charming, beautiful.

Ruchita: shining, desired, bright.

Rudrata: roaring.

Rukma: sun, radiant.

Rūpavān: possessed with beauty, handsome.

Rūpāvat: possessed with beauty, handsome.

Rupendra: lord of form, eye.

Rupesh: lord of form.

Rupin: embodied beauty.

Rupīn: with a beautiful form.

Rushat: brilliant, bright, shining, white.

Russel: red-haired, fox-like.

Rutajit: conquerer of truth.

Rutva: speech, intensity.

Rumalā: like salt.

Rupānga: beautiful salt.

Ruraka: wild.

Rushadru: who removes anger.

Rushangu: with white cow.

Rusheku: with a brilliant chariot.

S

Sabal: strong.

Sabar: milk.

Sabhajit: honoured, celebrated, praised.

Sabhavān: effecting welfare, Shiva.

Sabhya: refined, cultured, noble.

Sacchil: virtuous, of good character.

Sacchit: pure existence, pure thought, Brahma.

Sachan: ready to befriend, kindly-disposed.

Sāchār: well-behaved, well-conducted.

Sāchāru: very beautiful.

Sacheev: friend, helper, companion.

Sachetan: awake, rational.

Sāchi: following, accompanying.

Sachin: pure existence, affectionate, Shiva.

Sachint: thoughtful.

Sachit: wise.

Sachitta: blessed with reason.

Sadājit: eternally victorious.

Sadakānt: always loved.

Sadal: with petals, flower.

Sadānand: eternal bliss, Shiva.

Sādar: showing respect, considerate, attentive, beloved.

Sadāshiv: ever kind, ever prosperous, always happy.

Saday: kind, merciful, compassionate.

Saddhan: prosperous, wealthy.

Saddhee: wise, sage.

Sadguru: good teacher.

Sadhan: wealthy, possessing, devotion.

Sadhanee: companion, comrade, friend.

Sadhee: blessed with reason.

Sādhilā: mastered, accomlished, perfected, subdued.

Sadheeman: full of intelligence.

Sādhiman: goodness, excellence, perfection.

Sādhin: acomplishing, performing.

Sādhij: well-born, good conduct.

Sādi: having a beginning.

Sadiv: eternal like truth.

Sadman: abode, temple.

Sādyant: from beginning to end, complete, entire.

Sagaṇ: with troops, attended by followers, leader, Shiva.

Sagar: full of moisture, accompanied by eulogy, poisonous, air, atmosphere.

Sāgar: ocean.

Sagardutt: gift of ocean.

Saguṇ: complete with virtues, virtuous.

Sāguṇya: excellence, superiority.

Sahaj: simple, natural, original, hereditary.

Sahajit: victorious immediately.

Sahamān: conquering, victorious.

Sāhanja: easily won.

Sahānya: mighty mountain.

Sahar: like Shiva, Shiva.

Sahari: like Hari (Shiva), lion, bull, sun.

Saharsha: joyful, glad.

Sahasān: mighty, powerful, sacrifice, peacock.

Sahasin: powerful, mighty.

Sahaskrit: bestowing power, bestowing strength.

Sahasrajit: conqueror of thousands, Vishnu.

Sahastrabahu: one with thousand arms, lord Shiva.

Sahasvat: full of valour, mighty, powerful, victorious.

Sahasya: mighty, strong.

Sahat: mighty, strong.

Sahāvan: having strength, mighty.

Sahāy: accompaning, companion, helper, Shiva.

Sahil: flowing, water.

Sahir: mountain.

Sahishnu: patient, forbearing, enduring, Vishnu.

Sahishṭha: most powerful, strongest.

Sāhlād: joyous, cheerful.

Sahoj: full of strength, produced by strength.

Sahojit: victorious due to strength.

Sahor: excellent, good, pious, saint.

Sahovan: mighty, superior.

Sahuri: hot, mighty, strong, victorious, sun.

Sahvan: powerful, mighty.

Sahya: able to bear, agreeable, powerful, strong.

Sahyu: conquering, victorious.

Saif: sword of religion.

Sailesh: the Almighty.

Sajeel: beautiful, handsome.

Sajeev: full of life, alive, living.

Sajitvan: victorious, superior.

Sajjan: noble, respectable, well-born, gentleman, guard, sentry.

Sakal: all, whole, complete, full, perfect, universe.

Sakaladeep: illuminator of all.

Sakalendu: full moon.

Sākār: having form, beautiful.

Sākāsh: with light shining.

Sakraj: Indra's son.

Saksham: able, powerful.

Sāl: water, moving, dog.

Salaj: water which flows from melted ice from mountain.

Salay: friend, helper, Shiva.

Salil: water.

Salilesh: lord of waters.

Salin: worth appreciating.

Salmān: protector.

Sama: equal, smooth, even, flat, honest, just, peace.

Samādar: great respect, veneration.

Samaja: forest, multitude.

Samak: peacemaker.

Samālya: garlanded, crowned.

Sāman: calming, tranquillising, chanted hymn, song of praise, destroying sin, affluent.

Samān: equal, similar, identical, possessing honour.

Samang: with balanced features.

Samangal: auspicious, full of happiness.

Samanjas: correct, excellent, good, proper, right, sound, fit, Shiva.

Sāmant: limiting, bordering, leader, general, companion.

Samar: confluence, concourse.

Sāmar: accompanied by Gods, with the immortals.

Samarchak: worshipping.

Samardhan: causing to prosper.

Samarendra: lord of war, Lord Vishnu.

Samarjit: victorious in war.

Samarth: capable.

Samay: season, time, coming together, covenant, direction, limit, order, speech.

Sambhā: shine fully, be visible, be very bright.

Sambhar: supporter, bestower, bringing together.

Sambhav: meeting, ability, birth, creation, origin, intimacy, union, manifestation.

Sambodh: perfect knowledge.

Samedh: full of strength.

Sameech: ocean, sea.

Sameek: vanquisher of peace, fight, conflict.

Sameer: set in motion, create, urge on, air, wind, Shiva.

Samendra: lord of equality.

Samesh lord of equality, like Gods.

Samik: calm, tranquil.

Samin: achiever of peace, pacific, tranquil, consoler.

Sammad: joy, exhilaration, happiness.

Sammat: agreed, consented, esteemed, highly respected.

Sammiddha: full, complete, ignited, perfect, inflamed.

Sammit: measured, symmetrical.

Sammod: fragrance.

Sammohan: bewildering, bewitching.

Sammud: joy, delight.

Sāmod: full of joy, pleasant, fragrant.

Sampār: accomplished, fulfilled.

Sampat: fortune, wealth, welfare, prosperity.

Sampāti: flying, encounter, confluence.

Sampāvan: perfect purification.

Samprati: in the proper way, just at present, now, righteous.

Sampreet: totally contented, pleased, happy.

Samrāj: ruling over all, universal ruler.

Sämrāṭ: universal, supreme ruler.

Samriddh: perfect, complete, whole, abundant, accomplished, wealthy.

Sāmrit: provided with nectar.

Samud: full of joy, joyful, happy.

Samvar: satisfied, fulfilled, contented, best in every respected.

Sānag: beautiful mountain, preceptor.

Sanaj: ancient.

Sanak: old, ancient, former.

Sānal: full of fire, fiery, powerful, vigorous.

Sanan: gaining, acquiring.

Sānand: full of joy, glad, delighted.

Sanandan: joyful.

Sanas: smiling, laughing.

Sānasi: bringing wealth, bringing blessings.

Sanat: eternal, ever, perpetual, Brahma.

Sanātan: eternal, perpetual, permanent,

ancient, Brahma, Vishnu, Shiva.

Sanāth: with a protector.

Sanchitta: even-minded, equable.

Sandeep: blazing, burning, glowing.

Sandesh: message.

Sandeepan: exciting, inflaming, arousing.

Sandhā: promise, ultimate union, compact.

Saneehār: liberal, bestowing gifts.

Sanemi: complete, perfect.

Sanesh: army commander.

Sangat: getting together, suitable, proper, fit, consistent, compatible.

Sangav: afternoon.

Sanheet: collection of hymns.

Sanil: gifted, rewarded.

Sanjay: completely, victorious, triumphant.

Sanjeed: serious, peaceful, wise.

Sanjeev: possessed with life, luring, existing.

Sanjit: perfectly victorious.

Sanjog: coincidence.

Sankish: Lord, God.

Sankit: possessed with fire, burning torch, firebrand.

Sankram: progress, transition, shooting star, bridge.

Sankriti: arranger.

Sānkur: budding, having shoots.

Sannati: sound, humility.

Sanrāg: redness, passion, vehemence.

Sanrāj: reign universally.

Sanshray: asylum, shelter, aim, alliance, association, connection.

Sanshubh: radiant, handsome, beautiful.

Santosh: satisfaction.

Santya: bestowing, gifts, generous, kind.

Sānug: with attendants, with followers.

Sāmurāg: affectionate, passionate.

Sanyam: effort, control, self-restraint.

Sanyāti: coming, following.

Sapan: dream.

Saparyu: devoted, faithful, honouring.

Sarāg: having colour, passionate.

Saraj: water-born, lotus.

Saral: frank, candid.

Saran: moving, running.

Sarang: dappled, low, earth, gold, jewel, night, ornament, peacock, sandalwood, light.

Saranyu: fleet-footed, nimble, quick, cloud, wind, water, spring.

Sāras: coming from a lake, moon, Indian crane.

Sārasam: lotus.

Sarasij: originating in water, lotus.

Sarashmi: radiant, with rays.

Sarasvat: learned.

Sarasvat: abounding in lakes, related to water, juicy.

Sarayu: moving fast, air, wind.

Sārchi: burning, flaming.

Sārdūla: lion, tiger, the best, eminent.

Sareen: approaching, helpful.

Sargam: going smoothly, musical notes.

Saril: bringer of essence, water.

Sāriman: going, wind.

Sarjū: going, following, merchant, necklace.

Sarka: air, wind, mind.

Saroj: produced in lakes, lotus.

Saruchi: having splendour.

Sarūp: uniform, beautiful, embodied, handsome.

Sarur: happiness, delight.

Saruru: heart of the pond, lotus.

Sarva: whole, entire, various.

Sarvad: all-bestowing, Shiva.

Sarvag: all-pervading, omnipresent, soul, spirit, Shiva.

Sarvagat: all that exists.

Sarvahit: useful to all.

Sarvajit: all-conquering.

Sarvak: all, whole, entire.

Sarvān: a sage's son.

Sarvang: perfect in limb, complete, Shiva.

Sarvashay: refuge of all, Shiva.

Sarvesh: lord of all.

Sarvoday: upliftment of all.

Sasār: having strength, energetic.

Sasmit: accompanied with smiles, smiling.

Sasur: with gods.

Satachit: existence, thought, Brahma.

Satanām: name of truth.

Saleen: real, essential.

Sateendra: lord of Sati, Shiva.

Sateesh: lord of Sati (Durga), Shiva.

Satishay: best, superior, eminent.

Satkār: virtuous deed.

Satkrita: doer of virtuous deeds, honoured, respected, adored, Shiva.

Satman: with a soul, united with Supreme Spirit.

Satpati: true lord, champion, leader, good lord.

Sattva: being, existence, essence, energy, life, reality, courage, determined.

Satvat: full of truth, faithful.

Sātvat: full truth, pleasant, delighted.

Sātvik: virtuous, essence, good, real.

Satvindra: lord of virtue.

Satya: true, real, pure, virtuous.

Satyadarshi: one who can see the truth.

Satyaj: born of truth, of true nature.

Satyajit: victory of truth.

Satyajyot: lamp of truth, leading on to path of truth.

Satyakām: desirer of truth, seeker of truth.

Sātyaki: truthful, faithful.

Satyam: truth, honest, virtuous.

Satyamurty: statue of truth.

Satyanarayan: lord Vishnu.

Satyaprakash: light of truth.

Satyasār: essence of truth.

Satyasheel: of a virtuous disposition, very virtuous, pious.

Satyashree: glory of truth, best among the truthful.

Satyavan: one who speaks truth.

Satyavrat: one who has taken the vow of truth.

Satyen: truthful.

Satyendra: best among the truthful.

Satyeshu: desirer of truth, truth-seeker.

Saubal: full of power, very powerful.

Sauman: flower.

Saumya: related to moon, auspicious, brilliant, gentle, handsome, pleasing, mild, soft.

Saura: divine, celestial, sacred to the sun.

Saurabh: fragrant.

Saurav: sweet-sounding.

Saurik: celestial, heavenly.

Sauvān: celestial, heavenly.

Savai: instigator, stimulator.

Sāvant: employer.

Savās: scented, fragrant.

Savitar: sun.

Savitendra: sun.

Sawyer: woodsman.

Sayan: binding.

Sāyan: having arrows, companion.

Sayanti: controlling.

Sayuj: united, companion, comrade.

Scully: town crier.

Sean: God's grace.

Sechak: sprinkler, cloud.

Seemant: boundary, limit.

Seerat: nature.

Seetesh: lord of Sita, Rama.

Senajit: conquerer of an army.

Seyan: obtaining, achieving.

Shabalā: spotted, variegated.

Shabast: born with armour.

Shadri: cloud, hovering like thundercloud over enemies.

Shadru: falling, Vishnu.

Shagmā: mighty, powerful, effective, friendly, kind. mountain, elephant.

Shagun: auspicious, lucky omen.

Shagurikā: capable, energetic.

Shail: mountain.

Shaildhar: one who holds mountain (Lord Krishna).

Shailendra: lord of mountain.

Shailesh: lord of mountains.

Shailūsh: actor, dancer.

Shaiva: sacred to Shiva, follower of Shiva.

Shāka: aid, help, herb, might, power, vegetation.

Shakadal: fragment of power.

Shakar: grateful.

Shakat: cart, weapon.

Shākin: helpful, powerful.

Shakra: strong, mighty, powerful.

Shakta: competent, capable.

Shaktidhar: powerful one, Kartikeya.

Shaktik: powerful, mighty.

Shakun: prodigy.

Shakuni: large bird, peacock.

Shakunt: bird, blue joy.

Shākvar: mighty, powerful, strong.

Shakya: possible, within reach.

Shāla: wall, fence, rampart

Shalabh: grasshopper.

Shalil: nice, good.

Shālin: possessing a house, praiseworthy, river, civet.

Shālu: perfume, lotus root, frog.

Shalya: arrow, dart, javelin, spear, boundary, fence, porcupine.

Shām: calmness, equanimity.

Shamak: peacemaker, pacifier.

Shamat: residing in peace, calm, tranquil.

Shambar: made of iron, best, cloud, excellent, fight, war.

Shambhav: peacefully born.

Shambhu: causing happiness, existing for happiness, benevolent, helpful, kind, Shiva, Vishnu, Brahma.

Shamee: effort, toil, work.

Shameek: peaceful, self-restrained.

Shamen: safe, delighted, prosperous.

Shami: fire, name of a tree.

Shamin: tranquil, peaceful, self-controlled.

Shammad: conqueror of ego.

Shammi: peaceful, tranquil.

Shampak: created by thunderbolts, shining as lightning.

Shamvat: auspicious, prosperous.

Shān: prestige.

Shanak: one who walks slowly.

Shankan: causing awe.

Shankar: causer of tranquillity, auspicious, prosperious.

Shankhapani: same as Shankhadhar.

Shankhdhar: one who carries a conch shell (Lord Vishnu).

Shankhi: ocean, Lord Vishnu.

Shankhin: possessor of conch, possessor of pearls, bearer of shells, ocean, Vishnu.

Shanku: arow, dart, javelin, spear, spike, weapon.

Shantam: most beneficent.

Shantanu: wholesome.

Shāntiv: bearer of peace, beneficient, friendly, kind.

Shanyu: beneficient, benevolent, fortunate, happy.

Sharad: autumn.

Sharak: born in reeds.

Sharan: auspicious, safety, protecting.

Shārangin: archer, bowman, defending, earth.

Sharanmegh: autumn cloud.

Sharañya: giving shelter, giving help, Shiva.

Sharañyū: defender, protector, cloud, wind.

Sharat: autumn, cloud, wind.

Sharatchandra: moon in Sharad season.

Sharavindu: genius.

Shardhat: bold, daring, defiant.

Shardul: tiger.

Sharmad: conferring happiness, making prosperious, propitious.

Sharman: shelter, protection, joy, delight, bliss, happiness.

Sharmañya: giving shelter, protector.

Sharmeel: bashful, modest.

Sharmin: auspicios, fortunate, happy.

Sharu: arrow, dart, missile, passion, partridge.

Sharvareesh: lord of might, moon.

Sharvat: bearer of arrows.

Shashānk: moon.

Shasheesh: lord of moon, Shiva.

Shashi: moon.

Shashibhushan: one who wears moon as ornament (Lord Shiva).

Shashidev: lord of moon.

Shashidhar: one who carries moon (Lord Shiva).

Shashikānt: moon-loved, moonstone.

Shashikar: moonbeam.

Shashikirañ: moonbeam.

Shashin: moon.

Shashipushpa: lotus.

Shashishekhar: one with moon at the top of head - Lord Shiva.

Shashwat: ever lasting, continuous.

Shasman: invocation, praise.

Shāsta: ruler, punisher, chastiser.

Shāstri: ruler, teacher, punisher, sword.

Shashvat: perpetual, eternal, numerous.

Shāshvat: eternal, constant.

Shatajit: conqueror.

Shatānand: delighting hundreds, Vishnu, Krishna.

Shatik: brave, bold.

Shatrajit: ever victorious.

Shatrughna: destroyer of enemies, Lord Ramạs brother.

Shatrujay: conquering enemy.

Shatrujit: conquering enemies.

Shatrunjay: conquering enemy.

Shaurav: belongng to the brave.

Shauri: heroic, of the brave, sun, Vishnu, Krishna.

Shaurya: heroism, prowess, valour, might.

Shausā: praise, eulogy, desire, wish.

Shavakrit: maker of corpses, Krishna.

Shavas: heroism, might, power, prowess, valour, might.

Shayu: resting, reclining, sleeping.

Sheeghra: quick, speedy, swift.

Sheeghrag: moving quickly.

Sheel: rock.

Sheetal: cool, cold, calm, gentle, passionless, wind, moon.

Sheetanshu: cool-rayed, moon.

Shekhar: head crown, diadem, crest, peak, best, chief.

Sheldon: protected hill.

Shelvarāj: most handsome.

Sheridan: wild man.

Sherman: wool cutter.

Sheshdhar: one who holds Shesha (snake) - Lord Shiva.

Shevār: treasury.

Shibi: palanquin.

Shikh: crest, peak, apex, pinnacle.

Shikhar: mountain peak.

Shikhin: crested, attaining the summit of knowledge.

Shikshitā: clever, docile, modest, skilful, studied.

Shikshu: helpful, generous.

Shikvas: able, mighty. powerful.

Shilin: rocky, mountain-like.

Shileesh: lord of the mountain, firm will.

Shilpi: artist.

Shineya: white, shining.

Shinhir: cool, cold, season, dew, frost, cold.

Shinshu: child, infant.

Shinsiranshu: having cold rays, moons.

Shipi: ray of light.

Shiprak: plough, sun.

Shirish: avacia tree.

Shisham: ashoka tree.

Shishir: winter.

Shishay: generous, benevolent.

Shishul: infant, child.

Shita: good-matured.

Shiva: in whom all things lie, auspicious, benign, dear, friendly, gracious, favourable, kind, propitious, one of the Trinity.

Shivakar: causing happiness, auspicious.

Shivam: of Shiva, auspicious, graceful, prosperous.

Shivanand: one who is happy in Lord Shivąs thoughts or Shivąs worship.

Shivashree glory of Shiva.

Shivkumar: son of Lord Shiva (Ganesh, Kartikeya) (Shivanandan).

Shivshekhar: one at the top of Shiva (moon).

Shobhak: brilliant, beautiful.

Shobhan: handsome, excellent, Shiva.

Shobhin: beautiful, brilliant, splendid.

Shobhit: adorned, beautiful, embellished, splendid.

Shonit: crimson.

Shoshan: absorption, draining, parching, drying up.

Shranth: binding, tying, Vishnu.

Shrava: loud praise, fame, glory, renown.

Shravaṅ: ear, hear.

Shrāvast: famous.

Shravojit: winning fame, glorious.

Shree: diffusing light, adorning, holy, sacred.

Shreedhar: possessor of fortune.

Shreeharsha: delighting in prosperity.

Shreeja: born of Lakshmi Goddess.

Shreekānt: beautiful-throated, Shiva.

Shreekar: causing prosperity, Vishnu.

Shreekrishna, Shrikrishna: Krishna.

Shreekumar , Shrikumar: beautiful.

Shreeman: bearer of prosperity, bearer of beauty and grace, fortunate.

Shreemant: pleasant, charming, glorious, royal, wealthy.

Shreemat: bearer of prosperity, auspicious, royal, charming, beautiful, glorious, pleasant, Vishnu.

Shreenāth: lord of Shree, Vishnu.

Shreeniket: abode of beauty, abode of Shree.

Shreenivas , Shrinivas: abode of Lakshmi (vaikunth, Vishnu).

Shreeshā: lord of fortune, lord of Shree, Vishnu, Rama.

Shreeshaila: divine rock.

Shreevās: abode of Shree, Vishnu.

Shreevatsa: favourite of Shree, Vishnu.

Shreshṭha: excellent, foremost, best, chief, Vishnu.

Shreyas: best, most beautiful, auspicious, excellent, fortunate.

Shringa: highest point, perfection, peak, horn.

Shringesh: lord of peaks, Shiva.

Shrinjay: giving victory.

Shrishta: creator, Brahma.

Shrutānt: limit of fame, most famous.

Shrutya: famous, glorious.

Shubas: fragrant, sweet smelling.

Shubhān: bright, brilliant, shining.

Shubhānan: with a beautiful face, good-looking, handsome.

Shubhāng: lovely limbs, Shiva.

Shubhāshan: good speaker.

Shubhasheel: with a good disposition.

Shubhasheesh: blessings.

Shubhāya: bright and beautiful, to become a blessing.

Shubhendru: lord of virtue.

Shubhra: radiant, beautiful, clear, shining, white, heaven, sandal.

Shubhri: bright, beautiful, shining, sun.

Shubhū: of excellent nature, good, powerful, strong.

Shubrānshu: white-rayed, moon.

Shuchi: shining, bright, clean, holy, innocent, honest, pure, radiant, virtuous, ray of light, true friend, sun, wind, moon, Shiva.

Shuchindra: lord of purity.

Shukāyan: resembling a parrot, with a bright path.

Shukla: white, bright, light, pure, Shiva, Vishnu.

Shukra: bright, clear, pure, resplendent, spotless.

Shukratu: doer of virtuous deeds, benevolent, pious, virtuous.

Shūra: brave, powerful, valiant, lion, tiger, warrior.

Shushil: air, wind.

Shushmi: wind.

Shvet: white, white horse, white shell, white cloud.

Shvetak: white cowrie, silver.

Shvetang: fair complexioned.

Shvetank: having a white mark.

Shwetambar: one who wearswhite clothes, Lord Shiva.

Shwetanshu: moon.

Shwetbhanu: moon.

Shyām: black, dark, blue, dark-complexioned, cloud, Krishna.

Shyāmak: dark.

Shyāmal: dark.

Shyamsundar: dark and handsome, Lord Krishna.

Siddha: accomplished, divine, effective, pure, perfected, sacred, successful, Shiva.

Siddhanath: Mahadev (Lord Shiva).

Siddhānt: established, doctrine, principle, moral.

Siddhārth: accomplisher of aim.

Siddhesh: lord of the blessed.

Sidhra: perfect, good, successful.

Sidhya: auspicious.

Simant: limit, boundary.

Sindhu: river, sea, ocean.

Sinivāk: illustrious teacher.

Sishnu: prepared to give.

Sitakar: white-rayed, moon.

Sitanan: white-faced.

Sitānshu: white-rayed, moon.

Sitaram: Sita & Lord Rama.

Sitesh: lord of Sita, Rama.

Sitiman: whiteness.

Smayan: smile, gentle, laughter.

Snehal: friendly.

Sohan: handsome.

Sollasa: rejoicing, delighted.

Somā: moon.

Somadā: like a moon, giver of peace, procurer of nectar.

Somadev: God of moon.

Somak: little moon.

Somāl: soft, placid.

Somāli: soft, bland.

Soman: sacrificer of some juice, moon.

Somanshu: moon ray.

Somendra: lord of soma, moon.

Somesh: lord of soma, moon.

Somin: lord of soma, moon.

Somkar: moon light.

Somnath: lord of moon (Lord Shiva).

Somprakash: moon light.

Sonal: golden.

Sonam: gold-like, beautiful, fortunate.

Soval: powerful.

Soven: beautiful.

Spencer: dispenser, keeper.

Sraja: garland.

Sridhar: wealthy person.

Srikant: lover of wealth.

Srinivas: abode of wealth.

Srinjay: a prince's name.

Sriram: lord Rama.

Sṭanforḍ: residence.

Sṭanley: from the rocky meadow.

Stav: praise, eulogy.

Stuvat: praiser, worshipper.

Suaksh: with good eyes.

Subal: very powerful, Shiva.

Suban: shining brightly, brilliant.

Subhadr: gentleman.

Subhāg: fortunate, wealthy.

Subhās: shining beautifully.

Subhash: well spoken, eloquent.

Subodh: intelligent.

Suchāru: very lovely, delightful, handsome, pleasing.

Sucheet: carefree.

Suchendra: lord of piousness.

Suchetan: very conscious, very notable.

Suchetas: extremely wise, intelligent, benevolent.

Suchir: of long duration, eternity.

Sudakshin: with an excellent right hand, courteous.

Sudama: meek or humble person, Lord Krishnạs pauper friend.

Sudānu: bounteous.

Sudarsh: beautiful in appearance, eye-pleasing, perceivable, conspicuous, lovely.

Sudarshan: fair, Vishnu's disc.

Sudāvan: good gift, auspicious present.

Sudesh: good place.

Sudeva: good Deva.

Sudhakar: mine of nectar, moon.

Sudhan: very wealthy.

Sudhāshu: nectar-rayed, moon.

Sudhar: abode of the good.

Sudhāsū: nectar-producer, moon.

Sudhin: auspicious day.

Sudhindra: god of wisdom.

Sudhir: very considerate, very wise, firm, resolute.

Sudhish: lord of excellent intellect.

Sudhit: well disposed; benevolent, kind, nectar like.

Sudeep: very bright.

Sudeepta shining brightly.

Sudesh: beautiful, elegant.

Sudiv: shining brightly.

Sugat: going well, well-endowed.

Sugati: welfare, happiness, bliss.

Sugatu: welfare, prosperity.

Sugavi: with a beautiful gait.

Sughosh: one with melodious voice.

Sugriva: one with graceful neck, king of monkeys.

Sugun: with good qualities.

Suham: measuring happiness.

Suhās: with a beautiful smile.

Suhit: beneficial, very fit, suitable.

Sujal: of good water, Indian lotus.

Sujan: nice person, benevolent, good kind, virtuous.

Sujat: belonging to a good clan.

Sujāt: well-born, noble, beautiful, fine.

Sujay: great triumph.

Sujit: great vanquisher.

Suka: air, arrow, wind, lotus.

Sukalya: perfectly sound.

Sukānt: very handsome.

Sukarma: one who does good deeds.

Sukendu: like the moon.

Sukesh: with beautiful hair.

Suket: with good intentions, benevolent.

Sukhdev: god of happiness.

Sukhwant: pleasure-giving, happy.

Sukrant: extremely beautiful.

Sukratu: doer of virtuous deeds, benevolent, pious, virtuous, Shiva.

Sukreet: gold, auspicious, generous, holy deed.

Sūktā: well-recited.

Sukul: from a noble family.

Sukumār: very tender, very delicate.

Sulabh: easy to get.

Sulalit: graceful.

Suma: moon, sky, camphor, flower.

Sūma: milk, water.

Sumad: clever, wise.

Sumāhu: glorious.

Suman: of nice disposition, of great heart, charming very thoughtful, handsome, flower.

Sumanas: of high intellect, pure-hearted, easy, agreeable, cheerful, benevolent, gracious, favourable.

Sumand: well decorated, very slow, watchful.

Sumant: easily known, friendly sentiment.

Sumantra: good advisor, following good advice.

Sumantu: well-known, invocation.

Sumanyu: generous.

Sumat: of good nature, highly intellectual, wise, benevolent.

Sumati: good mind, intelligence, kindness, devotion, benevolence.

Sumaya: intelligent.

Sumedhas: of high intellect, intelligent, wise, sensible.

Sumeru: very exalted, excellent, mountain, Shiva.

Sumesh: good ram.

Sumit: well-measured.

Sumitranandan: sons of Sumitra (Lakshman & Shatrughna).

Sunam: good name (fame).

Sunanda: pleasing, delighting.

Sunandan: happy.

Sūnar: glad, joyous, delightful, merry.

Sunay: best neeti, best path of life.

Sunda: one who shines, Vishnu.

Sundar: beautiful, handsome, agreeable, charming, noble, Krishna.

Suneet: well conducted, prudent.

Sunil: very dark, dark, sapphire, blue grass.

Sunny: of happy disposition.

Suparn: one with nice feathers (Garud).

Suprāt: beautiful dawn.

Suprateek: with a beautiful form, handsome, lovely, Shiva.

Supreet: very dear, cherished friendly, kind, lovely.

Suraj: sun.

Surājan: well illuminated, divine, good king.

Surajit: victorious over gods.

Suranjan: delighting greatly.

Suranjay: Manu's son.

Surasū: father of Gods.

Surat: well disposed, ender, calm, tranquil.

Surebh: five-voiced.

Surendra: chief of Gods.

Suresh: lord of Gods.

Surjeet: conquerer of the suras (sur - god, opposite of Asur(demon).

Surnath: lord Indra, lord of suras.

Suruch: fine taste, glorious, delighting.

Suruchi: with fine tastes, taking delight in.

Surūp: well-formed, learned, handsome, wise, Shiva.

Surūsh: shining.

Sūrya: sun.

Suryabhan: sun.

Suryakant: loved by the sun, a shining crystal.

Suryakānt: sun-loved, sunstone, sun crystal.

Sūryanshu: sunbeam.

Suryaprakash: sunlight.

Susham: very beautiful, very even.

Sushansa: saying good things, blessing.

Sushānt: very calm, placid.

Susheem: cold, moonstone.

Sushen: lord of waters.

Sushenta: ray of the sun.

Sushev: auspicious, very dear, kind, favourable.

Sushir: with a good head.

Sushit: very bright, white.

Sushil: good-tempered, amiable.

Susmit: with a pleasant smile, self-consciousness.

Sushok: shining beautifully.

Sushrat: very famous.

Sutam: best among the virtuous.

Sutanjay: winning, son.

Sutantu: with fair offspring, Shiva, Vishnu.

Sutanu: with a beautiful body.

Sutārā: divine star.

Sutir: hero.

Sutosh: one who becomes happy easily.

Suvāch: praiseworthy, sounding good.

Suvāh: enduring.

Suvan: sun, fire, moon.

Suvansh: with a good lineage.

Suvar: sun, light, heaven.

Suvās: well-clad, Shiva.

Suvela: still, quiet, tranquil.

Suvit: easy to tranverse, good path, fortune, welfare, prosperity.

Suvrat: very religious, ruling well.

Suyajan: Vasishta's son.

Suyam: easily controlled.

Suyash: good result, victory.

Suyashas: glorious fame, very famous.

Suyati: passion-controlled.

Swagat: welcome.

Swāmin: owner, lord, master, chief, Shiva, Vishnu.

Swapan: dream.

Swāpi: good friend.

Swapnesh: king of dreams.

Swapnil: seen in a dream, dreamy.

Sāman: rich, wealthy.

Sahat: strong.

Sahoran: best among all.

Saleela: sportive.

Sankata: danger.

Shakala: cart.

Shamaka: peace maker.

Shamen: joyous.

Swarāj: king of heaven.

Swaran: gold.

Swarchis: flashing beautifully.

Swarup: figure.

Swayambhū: self-existent, Brahma, Vishnu, Shiva.

Swayus: with full vigour.

Shameeka: fight.

Svanga: beautiful body.

Svara: sound.

Svarahat: very respectable.

Svojas: very powerful.

Svaksha: beautiful eyed.

Subbra: hole.

Svadhita: firm.

T

Tahir: holy.

Tāhir: chaste.

Taksha: cutting through.

Takshak: cutter, carpenter.

Talan: musician.

Tālank: endowed with every auspicious sign, Shiva.

Talava: musician.

Tālin: adorned with cymbals, Shiva.

Tāleesh: lord of the earth, mountain.

Tallaj: excellent.

Talun: young, youth, wind.

Talūr: whirlpool.

Tama: darkness.

Tamāl: dark-barked, mark on forehead.

Tamas: darkness, gloom.

Tāmas: dark, malignant.

Tameeshwar: lord of darkness.

Tāmir: pure, tall, stately.

Tamish: moon, god of darkness.

Tamoghna: destroying darkness, sun, moon, Vishnu, Shiva.

Tamohar: remover of darkness, moon.

Tamori: enemy of darkness, sun.

Tāmra: coppery-red colour, made of copper.

Tāmrak: copper.

Tāmras: day lotus, gold, copper.

Tana: offspring.

Tanak: reward.

Tanamay: embodied.

Tanas: offspring.

Tanaveer: strong, robust, enlightened.

Tanay: son.

Tanayut: wind, night thunderbolt.

Tanish: mighty, brave, active, gold, ocean, heaven.

Tanishṭha: smallest.

Tankshit: balance.

Tanmay: engrossed.

Tansu: decorative.

Tāntav: made of threads, son.

Tanu: slender, delicate, minute, little.

Tanūbhav: son.

Tanūj: born of body, son.

Tanūn: without body, wind.

Tanurja: with heat in today.

Tapan: illuminating, burning, sun, hot season, sunstone.

Tapankar: sunbeam, ray of sun.

Tapas: penance, ascetic, bird, fire, heat, meditation, merit, potential power, warmth, sun, moon.

Tapasvat: ascetic, hot, devout, pious.

Tapaswin: hermit, ascetic.

Tapeej: gem.

Tapendra: sun.

Tapesh: lord of penance, Brahma-Vishnu-Shiva, sun.

Tapishru: warming, burning.

Tapit: refined gold.

Tapoj: born from heat.

Taporāj: lord of austerities.

Tarachandra: star & moon.

Tārādeesh: lord of the stars, moon.

Tārak: saving, liberating, helmsman, astral.

Tārakit: star-spangled.

Taral: glittering, tremulous, main gem of a necklace, wave, ruby, iron.

Taran: raft, heaven.

Tarang: goes across, wave, billow.

Taraṇi: moving forward, qick, energetic, helping, sun.

Tarant: ocean.

Taraswat: quick, energetic, hero, courier, bold, falcon, wind, Shiva.

Tareesh: boat, raft, competent person, ocean.

Tārendra: prince of stars.

Taresh: god of the stars (moon).

Tarik: dark, dusky.

Tāriq: star.

Tarkesh: god of stars (moon).

Tarkeshwar: lord Shiva.

Tarosh: sea, heaven.

Tarpaṅ: satiating, refreshing, gladdening.

Tarsha: with a fine form, ocean, raft, sun.

Taru: quick, protecting.

Taruṅ: young, tender, new, fresh.

Tarunak: youthful.

Tarunendu: waxing moon, new moon.

Tarush conqueror, sun, desire.

Tathagat: Buddha.

Tatharaj: Buddha.

Taturi: conquering.

Taulik: painter.

Tautik: pearl.

Tavaleen: absorbed in God, with God in meditation.

Tavashya: strength.

Tavish: strong, energetic, courageous, gold, heaven, ocean.

Tayin: protector.

Teḍdy: guardian of property.

Teertha: passage, place of pilgrimage, way, ford, sacred object, a worthy person.

Teerthak: sanctified.

Teerthankar: creating a passage, ascetic, sanctified teacher, Vishnu.

Tej: light, lustrous.

Teja: glow, lustre, sharpness, protection, effulgence, strength, splendour, glory.

Tejal: bringing light.

Tejas: fiery energy, spiritual power, glory, authority, majesty, knife-edge, point of flame, splendour, light, brilliance.

Tejasvat: sharp-edged, bright, beautiful, glorious, spirited, splendid.

Tejaswin: brilliant, bright, energetic, dignified, famous, noble, powerful, splendid, respect, sharp.

Tejawant: glorious, strong.

Tejendra: glorious chief.

Tejit: sharpened, whetted.

Tejomay: radiance.

Tejonidhi: abounding in glory.

Tejorāshi: mass of splendour.

Tejorūp: consisting of splendour, Brahma.

Tennyson: son of Dennis.

Tevan: sport, garden, pleasure.

Thatcher: roof fixer.

Thorne: thorn tree.

Tigma: ray of light, fame, sharp, hot, scorching, intense, weapon.

Tijil: moon.

Tilak: ornament of anything, mark on forhead as adornment.

Tilakrāj: best king, ornament to kings.

Timin: large fish.

Timit: calm, steady, quiet, fixed, tranquil.

Tishya: auspicious, fortunate.

Titha: autumn, fire, love, time.

Titukshu: enduring patiently.

Tivikram: Vishnu.

Todd: fox.

Tomar: lance, javelin.

Tosha: satisfaction, joy, pleasure, contentment.

Toshin: satisfied.

Toshit: satisfied, pleased.

Toyesh: lord of water.

Trāman: protection.

Trevor: caution.

Tribhuvan: the three worlds.

Tridev: hindu Trinity (Bramha, Vishnu & Mahesh - the creator, sustainer, destroyer).

Tridhama: shining in the three worlds, Vishnu, Brahma, Shiva.

Tridosh: God.

Trilochan: one with three eyes (Lord Shiva).

Trilok: the 3 worlds (heaven, earth, hell).

Trilokchand: moon of the three worlds.

Tripta: satiated, satisfied.

Trivart: pearl.

Ṭruman: disciple.

Tugra: water.

Tuhar: darkness, dispeller.

Tuhin: cold, dew, frost, mist, moonlight, camphor.

Tuhinakar: cold-rayed, moon.

Tuhinānshu: cold-rayed, moon.

Tuka: young, youthful, boy.

Ṭully: peaceful one.

Tulasidas: servant of Tulsi (basil).

Tumit: peaceful, calm, qiuet.

Tungar: high, lofty.

Tungeesh: lord of night, sun, moon, Krishna, Shiva.

Tungesh: moon.

Turaj: moving quickly, mind, horse, thought.

Turaṅya: swift.

Turaṅyu: swift, zealous.

Turāshāt: overpowering the strong.

Ṭurner: carpenter.

Tūrṅi: quick, clever, expeditious, zealous, mind.

Turvash: overpowering, triumphant.

Turvasu: victorious.

Tūrvi: superior.

Tushār: cold, dew, frost, mist, snow, fine drops of water.

Tuṣhāragiri: snow mountain.

Tushit: satisfied, contented.

Tushya: satisfied, Shiva.

Tuvaṅi: victorious.

Tuvideshna: giving much.

Tuvijāt: of powerful nature.

Taviksha: powerful.

Tūyam: strong, quick, water.

Tvakshas: energy, vigour.

U

Ubā: wealthy.

Ubādāh: serves God.

Ubaid: faithful.

Ubaidāh: faithful, servant of God.

Uberṭo: shining of mind.

Uboro: excellence.

Ucchal: going up, mind, understanding.

Ucchārya: to be spoken, pronounced, uttered, having spoken.

Ucchat: verse, praise.

Ucchatya: deserving praise.

Ucchikha: blazing, brilliant, flaming, radiant, high-crested.

Ucchiras: high-headed, with head held high.

Ucchreya: high, lofty.

Ucchrit: raised, lifted, arising, growing powerful.

Ucchit: delightful, agreeable, fit, proper, right, pleasurable.

Udāchit: worshipped, raised.

Udaj: born in water, lotus.

Udam: duty.

Uday: born in water, lotus.

Udanchit: raised, worshipped.

Udant: good, virtuous, folktale, message, news, rest.

Udāpi: attainer, successful.

Udār: high, lofty, exalted, best, great, noble, gentle, generous, dignified, kind, illustrious, distinguished, splendid.

Udāradhi: with an exalted intellect, wise.

Udārak: excellent person.

Udārāsh: with generous eyes, merciful.

Udārathi: arising, Vishnu.

Udarachis: shining upwards, flaming, brilliant, resplendent, Shiva.

Udarsha: overflowing.

Udātta: high, lofty, dear, elevated, great, gift, illustrious, ornament, gentle, generous.

Udāvasu: treasure of nobility.

Uday: ascending, accomplishment, prosperity, splendour, rising sun, emerging, appearance, creation, production, success.

Udayāditya: sunrise.

Udayagiri: mountain of ascent, mountain of sunrise.

Udayan: rising up, sunrise, result, conclusion.

Udayant: risen, end of sunrise.

Udāyin: rising, ascending, coming forth, prosperous, flourishing, Vishnu.

Udbal: very strong, powerful.

Udbhāsh: radiance, splendour.

Udbhāsit: emerging, lit up, respendent, beautiful, adorned.

Udbhav: originate from, existence, origin, birth.

Uddālak: burnt open, honey.

Uddāma: flaring up, unrestrained, free, large, great, impetuous, extraordinary, unlimited.

Uddānt: humble, energetic, elevated, pure, virtuous.

Uddarshan: with clear vision.

Uddhav: raising, lifting up, spirited, festival, joy, pleasure, sacrificial fire.

Uddeep: illuminating, lighting up, inflaming.

Uddeepak: stimulating, inflaming.

Uddeesh: lord of divine beings, Shiva.

Uddyot: shining, flashing.

Udeeshit: risen, elevated.

Udeh: praised.

Udgat: risen, ascended, emerged, leader, priest, preceptor.

Udgeet: sung, celebrated, highly praised, hymn of glory, ultimate song.

Udit: risen, ascended, high lofty, tall, born, apparent, visible, produced, sunrise.

Udojas: very strong.

Uḍolf: prosperous, wolf.

Udrak: of water.

Udrek: idea, superiority.

Udvansh: of noble descent.

Udyat: rising, star.

Udyot: shining forth, light, lustre.

Ugam: rising upwards.

Ugrak: strong, courageous.

Ujās: light before dawn.

Ujesh: one who bestows light.

Ujjayant: having conquered.

Ujjesh: victorious.

Ujjwal:highly inflamed, bright, burning, beautiful, clean, clear, lovely, light, illumined, sunshine, love sentiment, splendid.

Ukshit: sprinkled, moistened, strong.

Ulhās: splendour, merriment, light.

Ulick: playful.

Ulrich: prosperity, power, wolf, ruler.

Umachandra: Uma (Goddess Parvati) and Lord Shiva.

Umakant: husband of Uma (Lord Shiva).

Umang: enthusiasm.

Umar: flourishing.

Umber: earth's colour.

Umed: hope.

Umesh: lord of Uma, Shiva.

Umit: hope.

Unicus: unique.

Unmaj: coming forth.

Unmesh: opening of eyes, flashing, blooming of flower, emerging, visible.

Unnat: elevated, raised, high, tall, great, noble, prominent.

Unnateesh: lord of prosperity, lord of progress.

Unwin: non-friend.

Upadeesh: suggested, showing, pointing out, beaches.

Upanandan: like a son, Shiva.

Upanāy: leader.

Upashānt: very calm.

Upanshu: chanting of hymns or mantras in low tone.

Upendo: love.

Upendra: element.

Uqbāh: end of everything.

Uraj: strong.

Uri: my light.

Uriāh: God is my Light.

Urien: privileged.

Urveesh: lord of earth, king.

Usāmāh: description of a lion.

Usham: summer.

Ushar[illegible]: with desire.

Uttambha: propping.

Uttansika: a snake adorn with a crest.

Utpāra: beyond horizon, endless.

Utpalin: plenty of lotus flowers.

Ushapati: husband of dawn (sun).

Ushenya: longed for, desired.

Ushika: dawn worshipper, early riser.

Ushir: a flower.

Usmān: baby bird.

Ustin: just, true.

Uthman: baby bird.

Utkarsh: prosperity, awakening.

Utkāsh: shine forth, flash, emerging.

Utresh: Shiva.

Utpal: blue lotus.

Uttam: best.

Uttānk: high cloud.

Uttānsh: ornament.

Uzi: God is my strength.

Utsāha: courage.

Utsarga: setting free, oblation.

Uttarāk: delivered.

Ushjala: water of dawn.

V

Vachan: declaration, oath, command, order.

Vāgesh: Brahma, lord of speech.

Vāhati: companion, wind, river.

Vāhi: carrying, bearing.

Vaibhav: might, power, glory, grandeur, greatness.

Vaidat: knowing.

Vaijayant: bestower of victory, banner, flag.

Vairāj: divine glory.

Vairāt: precious stone, earthworm.

Vaishravan: widely known.

Vajramani: diamond.

Vakshu: refreshing.

Vallabh: beloved, above all, desired, favourite, cowherd.

Vāma: lovely, pleasant, dear, noble, splendid, Shiva.

Vaman: short.

Vāna: intelligent.

Vanan: longing, desire.

Vanas: loveliness, longing, desire.

Vānce: dweller.

Vanchit: desired, wished, beloved.

Vandan: adoration.

Vaninath: husband of Goddess Saraswati.

Vanshaj: from a good family.

Vapun: formless, knowledge, God.

Vapush: embodied, wonderful, admirable.

Varan: native place.

Varārak: magnificent stone, diamond.

Varāroh: excellent rider, Vishnu.

Vareesh: sleeping on ocean, Vishnu.

Vāreesh: lord of the waters, ocean.

Varendra: sea, ocean.

Varesh: presiding over boons.

Varin: rich in gifts.

Vareeyas: excellent, best, Shiva.

Vārney: residence.

Varuṅ: all-enveloping sky.

Vāsan: perfume, fragrance.

Vasant: bestower of desires.

Vasātik: as bright as dawn, belong to dawn.

Vāsav: relating to demi-gods.

Vasava: lord Indra.

Vasesh: giver of boons.

Vashin: having will power, ruler, master, lord, master of one's passions.

Vasu: wealth, Lord Vishnu.

Vasudān: gift of the divine, donor of earth.

Vasudev: lord Krishnạs father, the God of wealth.

Vasuman: born of fire.

Vasumat: possessing treasure, Krishna.

Vasupati: rich man.

Vatsal: child-loving, affectionate with offspring.

Vaughn: little, small.

Ved: sacred knowledge.

Vedātman: soul of the *Vėda*, Vishnu.

Vedbhushan: one adorned with knowledge of the Vedas.

Vedeesh: lord of the wise, Brahma.

Vedhas: pious, holy, courageous.

Vedin: knowing, feeling, Brahma.

Vedprakash: light of Vedic knowledge.

Veer: brave.

Veerbhadra: the Ashwamedha horse.

Veerendra: lord of the brave.

Vehān: morning, dawn.

Venkaṭ: self-born, divine, naturally manifest.

Veṅu: bamboo, reed, flute, pipe.

Vibhakar: light-maker, creator of brightness, sun, five, moon, king.

Vibhas: illumined, deity.

Vibhav: companion, Shiva.

Vibhu: all-pervading, omnipresent, mighty, great powerful, strong, excellent, effective, eternal, Brahma, Vishnu, Shiva.

Vibhushan: ornament, adorning.

Vibhuvas: powerful.

Videep: shining forth, illuminating.

Vidit: known, understood, learnt.

Vidrut: with great speed.

Vidu: intelligent, wise.

Vidur: knowing, wise, learned, intelligent, skilled.

Vidush: wise.

Vidyacharan: learned.

Vidyadhar: demi - god.

Vidyādhar: receptable of knowledge.

Vidyākar: mine of learning.

Vidyānand: delight in knowledge.

Vidyārañya: pleasure in knowledge.

Vidyasagar: ocean of knowl-edge.

Vidyesh: lord of learning, Shiva.

Vidyot: shining, glittering.

Vidyut: flashing, glittering.

Vihāg: airborne, arrow, bird, sun, moon.

Vihān: morning, dawn.

Vijay: victory, conquest, triumph.

Vijayānk: mark of victory.

Vijayant: victorious in the end.

Vijayketu: flag of victory.

Viji: conquer, win, excel, defeat.

Vikās: brightness, light, radiance, growth, development, expansion, cheerfulness, serenity, appear, become visible.

Vikram: praiseworthy act, record, the sun of valor.

Vikramendra: king of prowess.

Vikrānt: courageous, bold, striding, victorious.

Vilās: brightness, light, radiance, growth, development, expansion, cheerfulness, serenity, appear, become visible.

Vimal: spotless, stainless, clean, pure, bright, transparent, white.

Vimaladitya: clean sun.

Vimalesh: lord of purity.

Vimalmani: pure jewel (crystal).

Vinay: taking away, leading, guidance, control, modesty, decency.

Vināyak: remover, leader, guide, lord of prayer, Ganesha.

Vindu: knowing, familiar with, acquiring.

Vindumān: knower, scholar, wise.

Vineet: tamed, trained, well-behaved, humble, modest, handsome, educated, neat.

Vinimesh: twinkle of the eye.

Vinod: sport, diversion, pleasure, pastime.

Vipan: sail, small trade.

Vipin: jungle, wood.

Vipinbehari: forest wanderer.

Viplav: drifting about, revolution.

Vipul: large, wide, thick, great, abundant.

Virāj: shining, brilliant, splendid, king, excellence, dignity, majesty.

Virāl: rare.

Virāt: grand, magnificent.

Virāv: echoing.

Virochan: moon, fire.

Vishal: huge, broad, great.

Vishnu: lord Vishnu, the preserver.

Vishnudutt: gift of Lord Vishnu.

Vishoka: griefless.

Vishrut: famous celebrated, pleased. delighted.

Vishwa: earth, universe.

Vishwajit: one who conquers the universe.

Vishwakarma: architect of the universe.

Vishwalochan: eyes of the universe (sun, moon).

Vishwambhar: all pervading one, Lord Vishnu.

Vishwamitra: friend of the universe.

Vishwanath: God of universe, Lord Vishnu.

Vishwankar: creator of the universe.

Vishwas: faith, trust.

Vishwatma: universal soul.

Vittanath: owner of money (Kuber).

Vitul: large, long, wise, thick, loud.

Vivek: judgement, ability to distinguish between good & bad.

Vratya: faithful.

Vrrija: strength.

Vrrikala: a garment made of bark.

Vrrisha: the zodiac sign of Tauras.

Vrrishaka: poisonous.

Vivekanand: joy of discrimination.

Viyam: stretch out, extend.

Vyomesh: lord of the sky, cloud & water.

Vrrishin: a peacock.

Vrrita: circle.

Vrritra: enemy.

Vyoman: heaven.

Vyombha: like heaven.

Vyusha: dawn, morning.

Vyushta: rising of the day.

W

Waḍe: ford.

Wādil: Allah's name (one of 99).

Wafeeq: successful.

Wāhi: messenger, Quran.

Wāhib: God, bestowed, munificent.

Wāhid: single, unequalled, exclusive, unique, peerless.

Wāil: coming back.

Wājeeh: noble.

Wakhab: Allah's name.

Walcoṭt: old cottage.

Walḍen: mighty.

Wāleed: newborn.

Waliyudeen: supporter of the faith.

Waliyullah: supporter of God.

Walker: cloth maker, tailor.

Waman: short.

Warren: watchman.

Wāseem: graceful, good-looking, handsome.

Wāshi: eagle.

Wāshingṭon: town near the water.

Wayne: wagon maker.

Websṭer: weaver.

Wells: from the spring.

Wes: west meadow.

Wilberṭ: trusted.

Wilfreḍ: much peace.

Williams: desiring, protector.

Winḍsor: river bank.

Wrighṭ: craftsman, carpenter.

X

Xachāry: remembered by God.

Xadām: earth, man.

Xālex: protector of mankind.

Xan: God is gracious.

Xander: protector of mankind.

Xandy: courageous, valiant.

Xanthus: fair-haired, yellow.

Xates: gatekeeper.

Xavier: bright, new house.

Xenon: stranger.

Ximen: obedient.

Xing: star.

Xuān: spring.

Xylon: forest-dweller.

Y

Yachary: remembered by God.

Yachnit: prayed for.

Yādav: descended from Yadu, Krishna.

Yadavendra: lord of the Yadavas, Krishna.

Yādeed: beloved friend.

Yadeesh: lord of marine animals.

Yadu: cowherd, founder of Yadava dynasty.

Yadunandan: Krishna.

Yadunath: lord Krishna.

Yagesh: Vishnu.

Yahav: swift, active.

Yahu: offspring, child, swift, mighty, strong.

Yāhyā: a prophet.

Yajak: worshipper, liberal.

Yakim: founded by God.

Yākub: supplanter, representative.

Yākun: precious stone.

Yale: fertile land.

Yaleb: faithful, bold.

Yaman: prayer.

Yāman: motion, course, invocation, prayer, march.

Yāmin: right hand.

Yamir: moon.

Yānis: gift of God.

Yanni: gift of God.

Yarād: flow, descent.

Yardān: king.

Yāred: descendant.

Yārin: understanding.

Yasār: ease, wealth.

Yāsashiku: gentle.

Yāseen: one of Prophet Muhammed's sons.

Yash: fame, glory, character, splendour.

Yashasvat: glorious, famous, splendid, excellent.

Yashodhar: maintaining glory.

Yashodhan: rich in fame.

Yashonandi: with happy fame.

Yashwant: one who has achieved glory.

Yashwanth: always famous.

Yashpal: protector of fame.

Yāsir: wealthy, rich.

Yatan: effort, energy.

Yateendra: lord of ascetics.

Yateesh: lord of ascetics.

Yaṭes: gatekeeper.

Yatin: ascetic.

Yātnik: making efforts.

Yavan: quick, swift, mixing, mingling, wheat.

Yāvinar: young.

Yaviyas: young.

Yayin: lord Shiva.

Yāzeed: grow, increase, enhance.

Yehudā: praised.

Yeshwant: success.

Yogeesh: lord of yoga, Shiva.

Yogendra: lord of yoga, Shiva.

Yogesh: lord of yoga, Shiva.

Yogi: devotee.

Yohance: gift of God.

Yonāh: dove.

Yonās: dove.

Yorick: farmer.

York: yew tree.

Yoshi: best.

Yudhajit: victor in war.

Yudhisthir: firm in battle.

Yue: moon.

Yul: past the horizon.

Yumā: son of the chief.

Yunus: a prophet.

Yuri: lily.

Yusuf: a prophet.

Yūval: brook.

Yuvan: young, strong, healthy, moon.

Yuvarāj: young king, crown prince.

Yuyutsu: eager to fight.

Yvonne: yew tree.

Z

Zāccheus: innocent.

Zāch: remembered by God.

Zackery: child of God.

Zāfar: companion.

Zāfid: bright, shining.

Zāfir: shining, bright, victorious.

Zāhi: bright, shining.

Zahid: self-denying, selfless.

Zāhir: shining, bright, associate, helper.

Zāhūr: flower.

Zain: beautiful.

Zakai: pure, innocent.

Zakariya: a prophets name.

Zakiy: pure.

Zāmin: security.

Zan: well-fed.

Zander: protector of mankind.

Zāreb: protector.

Zāred: trap, book.

Zāreh: protector.

Zāron: exalted.

Zashā: protector of mankind.

Zavād: present.

Zavier: bright.

Zayd: superabundance.

Zed: God is just.

Zel: bell.

Zen: religious.

Zenās: gracious.

Zenobio: strength of Jupiter.

Zephān: God's treasure.

Zephyr: west wind.

Zeth: investigator.

Zethro: abundant.

Zeus: powerful.

Zev: deer.

Zikr: reminder, mention, Quran.

Zimrān: praise.

Zinān: second son.

Ziven: life.

Ziyād: super-abundance.

Zoan: departure.

Zonās: dove.

Zūbin: toothy.

Zuhayr: bright, shining.

Zuki: bright.

Zūri: handsome.

Zyān: little king.

Some Special Names

Aadesh: message.

Aadhira: moon.

Aadi: important.

Aadil: justice.

Aamir: populous, full, prosperous.

Aarav: peaceful.

Aarif: acquainted, knowledgable.

Aarpit: to donate.

Aarush: first ray of sun.

Aaryan: illustrious.

Aasim: protector.

Aatish: fireworks, name of Lord Ganesha.

Abaan: old Arabic name.

Abbas: description of a lion

Abdullah, servant of God.

Abed: worshipper.

Abedin: worshippers.

Abezag: pure, holy.

Abheek: fearless.

Abhinay: expression.

Abhiraj: fearless king.

Abra: cloud.

Abrar: a truthful person, saint.

Acchutan: lord Vishnu.

Adeel: judge, honest.

Adham: black.

Adnan: proper name.

Afeef: chaste, modest.

Agasthya: a name of a sage.

Agrima: advance.

Ahmad: commendable, praiseworthy.

Ahren: enlightened.

Ahsan: nice, beautiful.

Akrash: attractive.

Akshun: a significant particle.

Akul: lord Shiva.

Ali: excellent, noble.

Alif: the first character in Hijaiyah.

Amalendu: pure like the moon.

Amalesh: pure.

Ameya: name of lord Ganesh.

Amjad: more Glorious.

Ammar: builder, constructor, religious person.

Amresh: lord Indra.

Amrish: lord Indra.

Amshu: atom.

Amshul: bright.

Amuk: some, one or another.

Anadi: eternal.

Anas: a group of people.

Anees: close friend.

Anesh: smart one.

Anikait: lord of the World.

Anirvan: undying.

Anirvinya: a name of God Vishnu.

Anjor: bright.

Ankush: control.

Anna: food.

Anram: continuous.

Anvesh: investigation.

Apoorva: not seen before, different, special, best, unmatchable

Appaji: lord Venkateswara of Balaji.

Aquil: wise.

Arinjay: victory over evil.

Aritra: one who shows the right path, navigator.

Arja: divine.

Arkaan: principles.

Arpan: offering.

Arsh: dominion, crown.

Arshad: heavenly.

Aryan: son of Arya.

Asad: lion.

Asher: happy.

Ashfaq: noble prince.

Ashit: lord of the rings - Saturn.

Ashneel: the best, unbeatable.

Ashraf: more honorable.

Ashwath: banyan tree.

Asif: forgivness.

Asjid: one who prays to God.

Ataa: gift.

Atal: unshakeable.

Atambhu: the holy trinity.

Atharva: name of Ganesha, the first Vedas.

Atif: generous.

Atimanav: super man.

Atraiu: great warrior.

Ausija: renowned, bright as the dawn.

Avanish: god of the earth.

Avasyu: lord Indra.

Avikam: diamond.

Aviral: continuous, ongoing.

Avtar: holy incarnation.

Awad: reward, compensation.

Ayaaz: respected and enduring.

Ayavanth: lord Shiva.

Ayman: lucky, on the right.

Ayoob: a prophet's name.

Azhar: the most shining, luminous.

Azzaam: determined, resolved.

Baahir: dazzling, brilliant.

Baasim: smiling.

Baha: beautiful, magnificent.

Bahuliya: lord Kartikeya.

Bakool: flower.

Banaj: lotus.

Banbihari: lord Krishna.

Bandhu: helper.

Bandish: binding, attach together.

Banke: lord Krishna.

Bankebihari: lord Krishna.

Bankim: lord Krishna.

Bansi: flute.

Banwari: lord Krishna.

Baran: noble man.

Barid: cloud.

Basaam: smiling.

Basel: brave.

Bashaar: bringer of glad tidings.

Batuk: boy.

Bhagirath: a pious king.

Bhagyaraj: lord of faith.

Bharadwaj: a sage.

Bheru: friend.

Bhishma: teacher of Kauravas.

Bhudhav: lord Vishnu.

Bhumi: earth.

Bhuvanesh: lord Vishnu.

Biboswan: Sun God.

Bigul: musical instrument.

Bilal: the prophet's person calling prayer.

Bimal: pure.

Bimb: halo.

Bir: courageous.

Biraj: to have a presence, to know one's self.

Birbal: brave heart.

Bishir: joy.

Bisujaksha: lord Vishnu.

Bunny: cute like rabbit (per name)

Chahel: good cheer.

Chain: peace.

Chakradev: lord Vishnu.

Chakradhar: lord Vishnu.

Chakravarthi: king.

Champak: flower.

Chanakya: bright.

Chandran: moon.

Chatresh: lord Shiva.

Chatura: clever.

Chhatrabhuj: lord Vishnu.

Chikku: sweet, fruit.

Chinkoo: chinky (round) face.

Chinmayu: supreme consciousness.

Chirag: lamp, deepak.

Chiranjiv: immortal.

Chitesh: lord of the soul.

Cole: prince of red roses.

Daiwik: by the grace of God.

Dakshesh: lord Shiva.

Danish: to be clever, mercyfull and forseening.

Danvir: charitable.

Dasharath: father of Lord Ram.

Dasharathi: lord Rama.

Dawoud: a prophet's name.

Dayashankar: merciful lord Shiva.

Debjit: one who has conquered Gods.

Devan: like a God.

Devang: from God.

Devank: godly.

Devbrata: Bhishma.

Deven: resembling a God.

Devpad: divine feet.

Dhairya: patience.

Dhanraj: king of wealth.

Dharmi: religious.

Dhimant: intelligent.

Dhir: wise.

Dhrupad: lord Krishna.

Dipendu: moon.

Dipesh: lord of light.

Diptanshu: sun.

Dipu: flame, light, shinning.

Divyesh: full of divinity.

Durijesh: moon.

Dwij: saint.

Dwijain: moon.

Dyumani: lord Shiva.

Eeshwar: God.

Ehimay: all pervasive.

Eka: Lord Vishnu.

Ekadant: lord Ganesh.

Ekagrah: focused.

Ekaling: lord Shiva.

Ekana: lord Vishnu.

Ekapad: lord Shiva.

Ekavir: bravest of the brave.

Ekavira: lord Shiva's daughter.

Ekbal: dignity.

Elavarasan: prince.

Emaan: faith.

Etash: luminous.

Evyavan: lord Vishnu.

Faaris: horseman, knight.

Faarooq: he who distinguishes truth from falsehood.

Fadl: outstanding, honorable.

Falgu: lovely.

Fanibhushan: lord Shiva.

Faris: perspicacity.

Fateen: clever, smart.

Fawad: heart.

Fidaa: redemption, sacrifice.

Fravash: guardian angel.

Fuad: heart.

Gadin: lord Krishna.

Gagnesh: lord Shiva.

Gajanand: lord Ganesh.

Gajrup: lord Ganesh.

Gandhi: sun.

Gandhik: fragrance.

Garry: spear.

Ghaalib: victor.

Ghaazi: conqueror.

Ghasaan: old Arabic name.

Ghiyaath: succorer.

Gian: master of knowledge, apostle of knowledge.

Girik: lord Shiva.

Gitesh: lord of geet.

Goraksh: lord Shiva.

Goral: lovable.

Gorav: lord Shiva.

Goutheesh: wisdom.

Govinda: lord Krishna.

Govindaraj: god Vishnu.

Grishm: heat.

Gul: flower.

Gulal: colour red.

Gunaja: virtuous maiden.

Gunamay: virtuous.

Gunin: virtuous.

Gurman: heart of the Guru.

Gurpreet: the loved one of the Guru or God.

Haamid: praising (God), loving (God).

Haani: happy, delighted, content.

Haarith: plowman, old Arabic name.

Haaroon: a prophet's name.

Haashim: generosity, prophet's grandfather.

Haatim: judge.

Hakesh: lord of sound.

Hammad: one who praises God.

Hamza: lion.

Hardik: full of love.

Harekrishna: lord Krishna.

Harendra: lord Shiva.

Haresh: lord Krishna.

Hariaksa: lord Shiva.

Harihar: lord Krishna.

Harikrishna: lord Swaminarayan.

Harindra: a tree.

Haris: protector.

Harjas: praise of the God.

Harjit: victor.

Harmendra: moon.

Haroon: hope.

Hasan: laughter.

Hasmukh: full of cheer.

Haytham: young hawk.

Hazrat: prophet/Jesus.

Hem: gold, lord Buddha.

Hemdev: lord of wealth.

Hemen: the king of gold.

Hemish: lord of the earth.

Hemraj: king of wealth.

Heramb: lord Ganesh.

Het: love.

Himalay: mountain range.

Himanish: lord Shiva.

Himanshu: moon.

Himmat: brave.

Hiresh: king of precious stones.

Hitendra: well wisher.

Hitesh: lord of goodness.

Hriday: heart.

Hrishi: pleasure.

Hritik: name of a Sage.

Hryday: heart.

Hrydayesh: lord of hearts.

Humaid: great.

Humam: courageous and generous.

Hunar: good qualities.

Husaam: sword.

Husnain: pure in the eyes.

Hussein: beautiful.

Idaspati: god of rain (Vishnu).

Idhant: luminous.

Ihsaan: beneficence.

Ijay: lord Vishnu.

Ikrimah: a female pigeon.

Ikshan: sight.

Ilisa: king of the earth.

Imdad: charity.

Imraan: a prophet's name.

Indravadan: lord Indra's name.

Indumal: lord Shiva.

Inoday: sunrise.

Ipil: stars.

Irenpreet: loving.

Irfaan: thankfulness.

Isaam: safeguard.

Ish: lord Vishnu.

Is-haaq: a prophet's name.

Ishayu: full of strength.

Ismaael: a prophet's name.

Jaabir: consoler, comforter.

Jaafar: rivulet.

Jag: ruler of the world.

Jagannath: lord Vishnu.

Jagdeep: light of the Universe.

Jagdeo: god of the world.

Jagish: lord of the Universe.

Jagjeevan: life of the world.

Jagmohan: lord Krishna.

Jagrav: awakened.

Jai: lord Shiva.

Jaideep: victory to the light.

Jaigopal: victorious lord Krishna.

Jairam: victory of lord Rama.

Jaisukh: happy victor.

Jaival: life giving.

Jaivardhan: lord Shiva.

Jaiveer: victorious.

Jalaal: glory of the faith.

Jalpesh: king of water.

James: a cheerful boy, he who supplants.

Janak: lord Buddha, father of Sita.

Janesh: lord of men.

Jaswant: victorious.

Jatan: nurturing.

Jawad: openhanded, generous.

Jay: victory.

Jayakumar: victory.

Jayesh: lord of victory.

Jerry: spear ruler.

Jhumar: child's play thing.

Jigar: heart.

Jignesh: intellectual curiosity.

Jina: lord Vishnu.

Jinadev: lord of victory.

Jinendra: lord of victory.

Jitesh: winner.

Jivaj: full of life.

Jival: full of life.

Jivraj: lord of life.

Joel: Jehovah is the Lord.

Jograj: lord Shiva

Joshua: funny, friendship, love.

Jugal: couple.

Jugnu: fire.

Jwalant: luminous.

Jwalia: lord Shiva.

Jyran: lost love.

Kaamil: perfect.

Kabir: famous poet.

Kalicharan: worshipper of Goddess Kali.

Kamesh: lord of love.

Kamlesh: the preserver, lord Vishnu.

Kampu: sweet.

Kanj: lord Brahama.

Kanu: lord Krishna.

Kanwaljit: lotus.

Kapoor: saffron.

Karan: instrument.

Kareem: generous, noble.

Karim: generous, a title of God, the merciful being.

Karmendra: god of action.

Karmjit: winner over obstacles.

Karnam: famed.

Kashi: luminous, pilgrimage spot.

Kashif: explorer, discoverer, revealer.

Kashinath: lord Shiva.

Kashyap: a sage and friend of Pandavas.

Kasish: lord Shiva.

Kathir: ray.

Kautik: joy.

Kavin: handsome, beautiful.

Keanu: cool breeze over the mountains.

Keshav: lord Krishna.

Keshto: lord Hanuman.

Ketav: another name of lord Vishnu.

Ketu: lord Shiva.

Kewal: only.

Khaleel: friend.

Khushal: happy.

Kinnar: singing gods in heaven.

Kirat: lord Shiva.

Kiratidev: lord of light.

Kireeti: another name for Arjun.

Kirin: poet.

Kirti: fame.

Kirtin: celebrated.

Kishan: lord Krishna.

Koshin: a delicate bud.

Krishang: lord Shiva.

Krishay: another name for lord Vishnu.

Kritanu: skilled.

Krithinidhi: fame and wealth.

Kritika: well starred.

Krivi: lord Shiva.

Kshantu: patient.

Kshiraj: nectar.

Kshrugal: a name of God Shiva.

Kuber: god of wealth.

Kulbhushan: pride of the house.

Kuldeep: light of the house.
Kumaran: lord Muraga, son of Sivan.

Kunda: lord Vishnu.

Kuntal: rice.

Kunwar: prince.
Kush: sacred grass.

Kushanu: fire.

Kushik: grandfather of Rishi Vishwamitra/ Saint.

Kusumesh: lord of flowers.

Kuval: wisdom.

Labeeb: sensible, intelligent.

Lahar: wave.

Lakhan: lord Ramạ's brother.

Lakshay: target.

Lalam: jewel.

Lali: blushing.

Lambodhar: lord Ganesh.

Laniban: lord Shiva.

Lankesh: Ravan.

Larraj: a sage.

Laven: fragrance.

Layak: capable.

Lekh: document.

Lemar: talented one.

Liladhar: lord Vishnu.

Lohendra: lord of three worlds.

Lohitaksh: lord Vishnu.

Loknath: lord Vishnu.

Luv: Ramạ's twin son.

Maahir: skilled.

Maalin: one who makes garlands.

Maalolan: name of deity in Ahobilam (AP).

Maazin: proper name.

Madhavan: lord Shiva.

Madhuban: lord Vishnu.

Madhuram: sweet.

Mahaketu: lord Shiva.

Mahakram: lord Vishnu.

Mahamani: lord Shiva.

Mahatru: lord Vishnu.

Mahavir: lord Hanuman.

Mahiraj: ruler of the world.

Mahmoud: praised.

Makeen: strong, firm.

Makrand: honey.

Malank: king.

Mamdouh: one who is commended, praised, glorified.

Mamnoon: trustworthy.

Mamraj: lord of affection.
Manesh: god of mind.

Mangesh: lord Shiva.

Manhar: lord Krishna.

Mani: gem.

Mannan: thought.

Mansour: aided (by God), victorious.

Mansukh: pleasing.

Mantha: another name for the sun, lord Shiva.

Mardav: simple.

Markanday: Shiva's devotee, a sage who wrote Devi Mahatmyam.

Martand: sun.

Maruti: lord Hanuman.

Marwan: old Arabic name.

Masoud: happy, lucky.

Mastikh: naughty.

Maulik: precious.

Maysarah: ease, comfort.

Meer: chief.

Meet: friend.

Meghaj: pearl.
Mehal: cloud.

Mikul: comrade.

Milan: meeting, joining.

Milit: comradship.

Misbaah: lamp.

Miten: male friend.

Mitrajit: friendly.

Modak: pleasing.

Modal: enjoyment.

Moh: love.

Mohak: attractive.

Mohul: attractive.

Moin: tell us.

Moksh: salvation.

Moosa: a prophet's name.

Mridul: soft, calm.

Mrigaj: son of the moon.

Mrigasya: lord Shiva.

Mritheya: having a lot of friends.

Mudil: moonshine.

Mufeed: useful.

Muhannad: sword.

Muhsin: beneficent, charitable.

Mukhtaar: chosen.

Mullinti: lord Shiva.

Munawar: bright.

Muneer: brilliant, shining.

Munish:lord Buddha.

Munjal: king of Gujarat.

Muntasir: victorious.

Munthir: warner, cautioner.

Muralidhar: lord Krishna.

Murtadhy: satisfied, content.

Musad: unfettered camel.

Mustafa: prophet Muhammad name.

Mutaa: obeyed.

Mutasim: adhering (to Faith, to God).

Mutazz: proud, mighty.

Mutee: obedient.

Muthu: pearl.

Naadir: dear, rare.

Naasih: advisor.

Naathim: arranger, adjuster.

Nabeeh: noble, outstanding.

Nabeel: noble.

Nabhan: noble, outstanding.

Nabhendu: new moon.

Nabhij: lord Brahma.

Nachiket: son of Vajashravas.

Nadeem: friend.

Naeem: comfort, ease, tranquil.

Nagaraj: king of cobras.

Naggar: lord Krishna.

Najeeb: of noble descent.

Namdev: lord Vishnu.

Nandish: lord of pleasure.

Nandu: one who always be cheerful.

Nanu: small.

Narayan: lord Vishnu.

Narayanan: title of Vishnu/ Krishna.

Narottam: lord Vishnu.

Narpati: king.

Naseem: fresh air.

Natheer: warner.

Natwar: lord Krishna.

Navdeep: new flame; new shine.

Naveen: new.

Navin: new.

Navraj: new rule.

Navrang: colourful.

Nawfal: generous, old Arabic name for the sea, rare.

Nazeeh: pure, chaste.

Neel: the colour blue.

Neil: blue.

Nibodh: wisdom.

Nihar: to admire.

Niket: home.

Nikhar: blossoming.

Nikolas: victory.

Nilesh: the dark lord, lord Krishna.

Nirad: cloud.

Niraj: lotus.

Nirav: silent.

Nirbhay: fearless.

Nirbhik: fearless.

Nishad: swar.

Nishat: a tree.

Nishesh: moon.

Nishthavant: trustworthy.

Niswarth: no selfishness.

Niteesh: god of Law.

Nitesh: master of the right path.

Nitin: new.

Nitish: lord Krishnas name.

Nityanta: lord Vishnu.

Nooh: a prophet's name.

Noori: shining.

Nridev: king amongst men.

Nripa: king.

Nripesh: lord of kings.

Numan: (Blood) Old Arabic name.

Ojayit: courageous.

Om: primordial sound.

Omeir: long living.

Omeshwar: lord of the Om.

Omkarnath: lord Shiva.

Ossama: one of the names of the lion.

Padam: lotus.

Padmayani: lord Brahama, Buddha.

Pankajan: lotus, lord Vishnu.

Panshul: lord Shiva.

Param: ultimate.

Paramahans: sadguru.

Paramjit: heroic.

Paranjay: lord of the sea.

Parimal: fragrance.

Paritosh: delight.

Parmeet: wisdom.

Parmesh: lord Vishnu.

Parvesh: lord of celebrations.

Pashupati: lord Shiva's incarnation.

Patag: sun.

Patoj: lotus.

Pavanaj: lord Hanuman.

Pehlaj: first born.

Phalak: sky.

Pinak: bow of Lord Shiva.

Pinakin: lord Shiva.

Pitambar: lord Vishnu.

Pogula: lord Venkateswara.

Poonish: lord of the pious.

Porush: man power.

Posh: month in Hindu calender.

Prabal: strong.

Prachet: lord Varun.

Pradhi: intelligent.

Pradhyumna: extremely mighty.

Pradyumna: god of love.

Pradyun: radiant.

Prakhar: smart.

Prakher: intelligent.

Prakhyat: famous.

Pramodan: lord Vishnu.

Pranad: lord Vishnu, lord Brahma.

Pranjivan: life.

Prasit: first ray of the winter sun.

Pratha: trend, custom.

Pratham: first.

Prathamesh: lord Ganesh, lord of the best.

Pravit: hero.

Premal: loving.

Pritam: lover, darling, loved one.

Pritesh: lord of love.

Prithish: lord of the world.

Priyam: beloved.

Pujan: the ceremony of worshiping.

Pukhraj: topaz.

Pulkit: happy, thrilled, over-joyed.

Purahan: lord Shiva.

Purajit: lord Shiva.

Purandar: lord Indra.

Purshottam: lord Vishnu.

Qays: firm.

Qudamah: courage.

Raahi: traveller.

Raakin: respectful.

Raamiz: symbol.

Raatib: arranger.

Rabah: gainer.

Rabee: spring.

Radhakrishnan: godess Radha and Lord Krishna.

Radhesh: lord Krishna.

Radhey: Karna.

Raed: leader.

Rafee: kind friend.

Rafey: pioneer.

Ragesh: the man who sings sweet ragas.

Ragheb: desirous.

Raghuveer: lord Rama.

Raj: rule.

Raja: king.

Rajab: the 7th month of the Muslim year.

Rajeet: decorated.

Rajendra: king of Gods, lord Indra.

Rajesh: king.

Rajit: brilliant.

Rakishi: wide load.

Rakshak: rescue.

Rakshan: lord Vishnu.

Ramadeep: lord Rama.

Ramadut: lord Hanuman.

Ramanuj: lord Krishna, lord Laxman.

Ranajay: victorious.

Ranjiv: victorious.

Rasbihari: lord Krishna.

Rashad: integrity of conduct.

Rashid: rightly guided, having the true Faith.

Rashmi: sun rays.

Rasmaru: lord Krishna.

Rasul: angel.

Ratish: lord of love.

Ratnabhu: lord Vishnu.

Ratnanidhi: lord Vishnu.

Raunak: pride and glory.

Ravin: sun.

Ray: beam of light.

Rayirth: lord Brahma.

Ricky: lucky.

Ridha: contentment.

Ridhwan: acceptance, good will.

Rikhil: eternity, eternal.

Rishit: the best.

Rishvanjas: lord Indra.

Roger: fame.

Rohiniraman: the enchanted Lord (Krishna).

Rohtak: sun.

Romir: interesting.

Ronak: celebration.

Rudra: lord Shiva.

Ruhan: spiritual.

Rukminesh: lord Krishna.

Rupeshwar: lord of the form.

Rushabh: decoration.

Rushi: saint, wise, advisor.

Rushil: charming.

Ruthvik: saint.

Rutveg: can travel in all climatic conditions.

Saabir: patient.

Saad: good luck.

Saahil: seashore.

Saahir: wakeful.

Saajid: one who worships God.

Saalih: good, righteous.

Saanjh: evening.

Saariyah: clouds at night.

Sabarish: lord Iyyappan.

Sabeeh: beautiful.

Sabrang: rainbow.

Sabyasachi: lord Arjun.

Sachchit: lord Brahma.

Sachet: consciosness.

Sachish: lord Indra.

Sachiv: friend.

Sadabindu: lord Vishnu.

Sadavir: ever courageous.

Sadeeq: trustworthy.

Sadgun: virtues.

Sadhil: perfect.

Sadru: lord Vishnu.

Saeed: happy, rivulet.

Safiy: best friend.

Sahas: brave.

Sahasrad: lord Shiva.

Sahishnu: lord Vishnu.

Sai: flower, everywhere.

Sajan: beloved.

Sajiv: lively.

Sakaleshwar: lord of everything.

Saket: lord Krishna.

Sakshik: witness.

Salah: righteousness.

Saleem: safe.

Salem: safe.

Salil: water.

Samaj: lord Indra.

Samajas: lord Shiva.

Samanyu: lord Shiva.

Samavart: lord Vishnu.

Sampathkrishna: a gift fom Lord Krishna.

Samdarshi: lord Krishna.

Samendu: lord Vishnu.

Samik: peaceful.

Samir: entertaining companion.

Samit: always making friends.

Samrudh: the enriched one.

Sanchay: collection.

Sanchit: collection.

Sandy: good lamp.

Sanjay: victorious.

Sanjiv: vital.

Sankalp: aim.

Sanket: signal.

Sannath: accompanied by a protector.

Santan: a tree.

Sanwariya: lord Krishna.

Saprathas: lord Vishnu.

Saptajit: conqueror of 7 elements.

Saptanshu: fire.

Sarin: helpful.

Sarish: equal.

Sarojin: lord Brahma.

Sarthak: having its own importance.

Sarvadev: lord Shiva.

Sarvadharin: lord Shiva.

Sarvambh: lord Ganesh.

Sarvavas: lord Shiva.

Sarvabhanu: name of sun.

Sarvendra: God of all.

Sashang: connected.

Sashwat: eternal.

Sasmit: ever smiling.

Satadev: God.

Satamanyu: lord Indra.

Satanand: lord Vishnu.

Satesh: lord of hundreds.

Sathi: partner.

Satin: real.

Satinath: lord Shiva.

Satkartar: lord Vishnu.

Satpal: protector.

Satrajit: ever victorious.

Satveer: lord Vishnu.

Satwaki: fighter.

Satyapramod: the true person Ganesh.

Satyadev: lord of truth.

Satyajit: victory of truth.

Satyak: honest.

Satyanarayan: lord Vishnu.

Saubal: mighty.

Saubhadra: Abhimanyu.

Saumit: easy to get.

Saumitra: Lakshman.

Saurjyesh: Kartikeya, the lord of Valour.

Savir: leader.

Savit: sun.

Savya: lord Vishnu.

Sayid: master.

Sehej: calm.

Senthil: lord Murugan.

Seshu: Seshanag.

Setu: sacred symbol.

Shaan: prestige, dignity, pride.

Shabar: nector.

Shafeeq: compassionate, tender.

Shahalad: joy.

Shahid: a martyr (religious or political).

Shakti: power.

Shalang: emperor.

Shaligram: lord Vishnu.

Shalik: a sage.

Shalina: courteous.

Shalmali: lord Vishnụ's power.

Shama: sun.

Shamak: makes peace.

Shamakarn: lord Shiva.

Shamir: rock that can penetrate metal.

Shamun: name of prophet.

Shankarshan: lord Krishnạ's brother.

Shankdhar: lord Krishna.

Shankhapani: lord Vishnu.

Shankir: lord Shiva.

Shantanav: Bhishma Pitamaha.

Shantidev: lord of peace.

Shantinath: lord of peace.

Shanyu: benevolent.

Sharan: shelter.

Shardul: the best.

Shareef: distinguished, noble.

Shashish: lord Shiva.

Shatrughan: lord Ramạ's brother.

Shauchin: pure.

Shaunak: wise.

Shazad: prince.

Sheece: prophets name.

Shibhya: lord Shiva.

Shighra: lord Shiva, lord Vishnu.

Shihab: flame, blaze.

Shikhandin: lord Shiva, lord Vishnu.

Shikhar: mountain, top of the mountain.

Shilang: virtuous.

Shineyu: shining.

Shipirist: lord Vishnu.

Shishul: baby.

Shitikanth: lord Shiva.

Shivadev: lord of prosperity.

Shivanath: lord Shiva.

Shivang: part of lord Shiva.

Shivank: mark of Lord.

Shivasunu: lord Ganesh.

Shiven: lord Shiva.

Shivendra: lord Shiva, lord Indra.

Shivendu: moon.

Shivesh: lord Shiva, Shiv+esh (Lord Shiys Ishwar Shri RAM.

Shiveshvar: God of welfare.

Shivraj: lord Shiva.

Shivram: lord Shiva; lord Ram.

Shlesh: physical bonding.

Shlokh: hymẹs of Lord.

Shoor: valiant.

Shrestajna: top knowledge.

Shresth: best of all.

Shresthi: best of all.

Shrey: marevellous.

Shrida: lord Kuber.

Shrigopal: lord Krishna.

Shrihan: lord Vishnu.

Shrihari: lord Vishnu.

Shrikeshav: lord Krishna.

Shrimohan: lord Krishna.

Shrinand: lord Vishnu.

Shriniketan: lord Vishnu.

Shripadma: lord Krishna.

Shripal: lord Vishnu.

Shripati: lord Vishnu.

Shriram: lord Rama.

Shrirang: lord Vishnu.

Shriranjan: lord Vishnu.

Shrivarah: lord Vishnu.

Shrivardhan: lord Vishnu, lord Shiva.

Shubendra: lord of virtue.

Shubh: fortunate.

Shubhaksh: lord Shiva.

Shubhankar: virtuous, lord Shiva.

Shubhojit: handsome.

Shulandhar: lord Shiva.

Shulin: lord Shiva.

Shuna: lord Indra.

Shvant: placid.

Shvetambar: lord Shiva.

Shvetanshu: moon.

Shvetavah: lord Indra.

Shyamantak: lord Krishna.

Shyamsunder: lord Krishna.

Siddhadev: lord Shiva.

Siddheshwar: lord Shiva.

Siddhraj: lord of perfection.

Siddid: lord Shiva.

Sindhunath: lord of the ocean.

Sinha: hero.

Sinhag: lord Shiva.

Sinhvahan: lord Shiva.

Siraaj: lamp, light.

Sivanantham: lord Shiva.

Smaran: meditation.

Smith: smile.

Snehakant: lord of love.

Sohail: moon-glow.

Soham: I am.

Sohil: beautiful.

Somanshu: moonbeam.

Somashekhar: lord Shiva.

Somasindhu: lord Vishnu.

Someshwar: lord Krishna.

Somnath: lord Shiva.

Soumil: friend.

Sourish: lord Vishnu.

Sravan: character in Ramayan devoted son.

Sridatta: given by God.

Sridhar: lord Vishnu.

Srinivas: lord Venkateshwara.

Sthavir: lord Brahma.

Sthir: focused.

Stimit: astonishing.

Stotri: lord Vishnu.

Subal: lord Shiva.

Subali: strong.

Subeer: courageous.

Subhang: lord Shiva.

Suchet: attentive, alert.

Suchir: eternity.

Sudama: lord Krishna's friend.

Suday: gift.

Sudesha: son of Lord Krishna.

Sudhang: moon.

Sudhanshu: moon.

Sudhanvan: lord Vishnu.

Sudhendra: lord of nectar.

Sudhindra: lord of knowledge.

Sudir: bright.

Suhail: name of a star.

Suhayb: of reddish hair or complexion.

Sujal: affectionate.

Sukhajat: lord Shiva.

Sukhakar: lord Rama.

Sukhashakt: lord Shiva.

Sukhdev: lord of happiness.

Sukhen: happy boy.

Sulayman: a prophet's name.

Sulek: sun.

Sulochna: beautiful eyes.

Sumatinath: lord of wisdom.

Sumed: wise.

Sumukh: lord Shiva.

Sunashi: lord Indra.

Sunay: wise, leader, a well conducted king.

Sundaravathana: smart and handsome.

Sunjeev: making alive.

Suparn: lord Vishnu.

Supash: lord Ganesh.

Suradhish: lord Indra.

Suradip: lord Indra.

Suragan: lord Shiva.

Surajiv: lord Vishnu.

Suram: beautiful.

Suran: pleasant sound.

Surarihan: lord Shiva.

Surbhup: lord Vishnu.

Suren: lord Indra.

Suri: lord Krishna.

Suryadev: sun God.

Suryesh: sun is god.

Susadh: lord Shiva.

Susen: lord Shiva, lord Vishnnu.

Susher: kind.

Sushim: moonstone.

Sutirth: lord Shiva.

Sutoya: a river.

Suvarn: lord Shiva.

Suvidh: kind.

Suvir: lord Shiva.

Suyamun: lord Vishnu.

Suyati: lord Vishnu.

Svamin: lord Vishnu.

Svaminath: lord Ganesh.

Svang: good looks.

Svanik: handsome.

Svar: lord Vishnu.

Svarg: heaven.

Svarna: lord Ganesh.

Svarpati: lord of sound.

Svayambhut: lord Shiva.

Swami: lord.

Swapnil: dreamy.

Swarit: towards heaven.

Swastik: auspicious.

Swayam: self.

Syon: gentle.

Syum: a ray.

Taamir: one who knows dates.

Taj: crown, jewel.

Taksha: king Bharat's son.

Taksheel: someone with a strong character.

Talaketu: Bhishma Pitamaha.

Talal: nice, admirable.

Talha: kind of tree.

Tamam: generous.

Tanav: flute.

Tanmay: reincarnated, concentrate.

Tanoj: son.

Tanvir: strong.

Tapeshwar: lord Shiva.

Tarakeshwar: lord Shiva.

Taraknath: lord Shiva.

Taraksh: mountain.

Taran: lord Vishnu.

Tareef: rare, uncommon.

Tarendra: prince of stars.

Tarfah: kind of tree.

Tathagat: lord Buddha.

Tatya: lord Shiva.

Tauheed: victoriuos.

Tawfeeq: success, reconciliation.

Taymullah: servant of God.

Tayseer: facilitation.

Tereshan: solid redemption.

Thaabit: firm.

Thaqib: shooting star.

Thavanesh: lord Shiva.

Tirishaanth: king of Surya dynasty.

Tirranand: lord Shiva.

Tirth: pilgrim.

Tirthankar: lord Vishnu.

Tirthayaad: lord Krishna.

Tisyaketu: lord Shiva.

Tonto: indulgence, devotion.

Triambak: lord Shiva.

Tridhaman: the holy trinity.

Tridhatri: lord Ganesh.

Trigya: lord Buddha.

Trijal: lord Shiva.

Trikay: lord Buddha.

Trilochan: lord Shiva (the three eyed).

Trilokanath: lord Shiva.

Trilokesh: lord Vishnu.

Triman: ruler of three worlds, worshipped in three worlds.

Trimurti: the holy trinity.

Trinabh: lord Vishnu.

Trinayan: lord Shiva.

Tripurajit: lord Shiva.

Tripurari: lord Shiva.

Trishar: pearl necklace.

Trishul: lord Shiva's trident.

Trishulank: lord Shiva.

Trishulin: lord Shiva.

Trivikram: a name of God Vishnu.

Tunda: lord Shiva.

Tunganath: lord of the mountains.

Tungeshwar: lord of the mountains.

Turag: a thought.

Tuvidyumna: lord Indra.

Ubay: old Arabic name.

Uchadev: lord Vishnu.

Udbal: mighty.

Uddiran: lord Vishnu.

Uddiyan: flying speed.

Uddunath: lord of stars.

Udu: water.

Udupati: lord of stars.

Uduraj: lord of stars.

Udyam: action.

Udyan: garden.

Ugresh: lord Shiva.

Ujendra: conqueror.

Ujjay: victorious.

Ulmuk: lord Indra.

Umaarah: old Arabic name.

Umair: old Arabic name.

Umakant: lord Shiva.

Umanand: lord Shiva.

Umang: happiness.

Umeshwar: lord Shiva.

Unnabh: highest.

Unnikrishnan: lord Krishna (baby stage).

Uppas: gem.

Uqbah: the end of everything.

Urav: excitement.

Urjani: lord of strength.

Urmiya: lord of light.

Urugay: lord Krishna.

Urvang: mountain.

Ushangu: lord Shiva.

Ushnisin: lord Shiva.

Utbah: old Arabic name.

Utkarsh: high quality.

Utpalaksh: lord Vishnu.

Utsav: festival.

Uttam: best.

Uttamesh: lord Shiva.

Uttar: lord Shiva.

Uttarak: lord Shiva.

Vachaspati: lord of speech.

Vadish: lord of the body.

Vagindra: lord of speech.

Vahin: lord Shiva.

Vaijayi: victor.

Vaikartan: name of Karna.

Vaikhan: lord Vishnu.

Vaikunth: abode of Vishnu.

Vainavin: lord Shiva.

Vairinchya: lord Brahma's son.

Vairochan: lord Vishnu's son.

Vaishvik: belonging to the world.

Vajasani: lord Vishnus son.

Vajendra: lord Indra.

Vajradhar: lord Indra.

Vajrahast: lord Shiva.

Vajrajit: lord Indra.

Vajrin: lord Indra.

Vakrabhuj: lord Ganesh.

Valmiki: saint who wrote Ramayan.

Vamadev: lord Shiva.

Vanad: cloud.

Vanadev: lord of the forest.

Vanamalin: lord Krishna.

Vanij: lord Shiva.

Vansh: coming generation of father.

Vansidhar: lord Krishna.

Varad: god of fire.

Varadaraj: lord Vishnu.

Varana: holy river.

Vardhan: lord Shiva.

Vareshvar: lord Shiva.

Varindra: lord of all.

Variyas: lord Shiva.

Varunesh: lord of water.

Vasavaj: son of Indra.

Vasavi: son of Indra.

Vashita: one who hypnotises by her virtues.

Vasudev: lord Krishna's father.

Vasupati: lord Krishna.

Vasur: precious.

Vasuroop: lord Shiva.

Vatatmaj: lord Hanuman.

Vatsa: son.

Vatsapal: lord Krishna.

Vatsin: lord Vishnu.

Vayu: lord Hanuman.

Vayujat: lord Hanuman.

Vayun: lively.

Vayunand: lord Hanuman.

Vayya: friend.

Vedamohan: lord Krishna.

Vedang: from the Vedas.

Vedant: Hindu philosophy.

Vedesh: lord of Vedas.

Velan: lord Shivạ's son.

Venavir: lord Shivạ's son.

Venkatesh: lord Vishnu, lord Krishna.

Viamarsh: lord Shiva.

Vibhavasu: lord Krishna.

Vibhor: ecstatic.

Vibhumat: lord Krishna.

Vibhushnu: lord Shiva.

Vibhut: strong.

Vibodh: wise.

Vidhatru: lord Shiva.

Vidhesh: lord Shiva.

Vidhu: lord Vishnu.

Vidojas: lord Indra.

Vidvatam: lord Shiva.

Vighnajit: lord Ganesh.

Vighnesh: lord Ganesh.

Vigrah: lord Shiva.

Vihang: a bird.

Vihari: lord Krishna.

Vijayendra: god of victory.

Vijayesh: lord Shiva.

Vijval: intelligent.

Vikhyath: fame.

Vikram: lord Shiva, record.

Vikramin: lord Vishnu.

Viksar: lord Vishnu.

Vikunth: lord Vishnu.

Vilohit: lord Shiva.

Vimridh: lord Indra.

Vinahast: lord Shiva.

Vinesh: godly.

Vinil: blue.

Vinochan: lord Shiva.

Vinoth: pleasing.

Vipaschit: lord Buddha.

Vir: brave.

Viraaj: king.

Virabhadra: lord Shiva.

Viranath: lord of the brave.

Virendra: lord of the heroes.

Viresh: lord Shiva.

Vireshvar: lord Shiva.

Virikvas: lord Indra.

Virinchi: Brahma.

Virochan: lord Vishnu.

Virurch: the holy trinity.

Visamaksh: lord Shiva.

Vishakh: lord Shiva.

Vishal: huge.

Vishalaksh: lord Shiva.

Vishantak: lord Shiva.

Vishatan: lord Vishnu.

Vishesh: special.

Vishnahpu: lord Vishnu.

Vishnu: a Hindu God.

Vishnusiddharth: lord Vishnu.

Vishnudev: God.

Vishodhan: lord Vishnu.

Vishresh: the holy trinity.

Vishvadev: lord of the universe.

Vishvadhar: lord Vishnu.

Vishvag: lord Brahma.

Vishvahetu: lord Vishnu.

Vishvajit: conqueror of the world.

Vishvaksen: lord Vishnu's names.

Vishvamitra: a sage.

Vishvanabh: lord Vishnu.

Vishvanath: lord of the universe.

Vishvaretas: lord Brahma, Vishnu.

Vishvas: faith.

Visveshwaran: lord Shiva.

Vitabhay: lord Shiva, lord Vishnu.

Vitaharya: lord Krishna.

Vitola: peaceful.

Vittesh: lord of wealth.

Vitthal: lord Vishnu.

Vivash: bright.

Vivek: intellect.

Vrajalal: lord Krishna.

Vrajesh: lord Krishna.

Vrajkishore: lord Krishna.

Vrajmohan: lord Krishna.

Vrajraj: lord Krishna.

Vratesh: lord Shiva.

Vriksh: tree.

Vrisa: lord Krishna.

Vrisag: lord Shiva.

Vrisan: lord Shiva.

Vrisangan: lord Shiva.

Vrisapati: lord Shiva.

Vrishab: excellent.

Vrishank: lord Shiva.

Vrisini: lord Shiva.

Vrushket: son of Karna.

Vyan: air.

Vyas: sage who wrote Mahabharat.

Vyoman: sky.

Vyomdev: lord Shiva.

Vyomesh: lord of the sky.

Vyshakh: vyshakh.

Waliyudeen: supporter of the Faith.

Waliyullah: supporter of God.

Waman: lord Vishnu's

name.

Yaaseen: one of the prophet Muhammad's names.

Yadunath: lord Krishna.

Yaduraj: lord Krishna.

Yaduvir: lord Krishna.

Yagna: ceremonial rites to God.

Yahyaa: a prophet's name.

Yaj: a sage.

Yajas: fame.

Yajat: lord Shiva.

Yajnadhar: lord Vishnu.

Yajnarup: lord Krishna.

Yajnesh: lord Vishnu.

Yamahil: lord Vishnu.

Yamajit: lord Shiva.

Yamir: moon.

Yashas: fame.

Yashneil: famous, glorious, successful.

Yashodev: lord of fame.

Yashpal: lord of fame.

Yashwanth: always famous.

Yatin: devotee.

Yayin: lord Shiva.

Yazeed: to increase, grow, enhance.

Yeshwant: success.

Yogi: devotee.

Yudhishthir: eldest Pandava brother.

Zackery: child of God.

Zakariya: a prophet's name.

Zayd: superabundance.

Zuhayr: bright, shining.

Top 50 boys' names in England and Wales

BOYS

1. Jack
2. Thomas
3. Joshua
4. James
5. Daniel
6. Harry
7. Saumel
8. Joseph
9. Matthew
10. Lewis
11. Luke
12. Oliver
13. William
14. Benjamin
15. Callum
16. George
17. Adam
18. Ryan
19. Jake
20. Alexnder
21. Ethan
22. Liam
23. Cameron
24. Connor
25. Jordan
26. Mohammed
27. Jamie
28. Dylan
29. Nathan
30. Jacob
31. Ben
32. Charlie
33. Michel
34. Kieran
35. Max
36. Bradley
37. Brandon
38. Owen
39. Louis
40. Aaron
41. Tyler (New Entry)
42. Kyle
43. Reece
44. Edward
45. Alex
46. David
47. Robert
48. Harrison (New Entry)
49. Christopher
50. Joe

Top 50 boys' names in Scotland

BOYS

1. Jack
2. Lewis
3. Cameron
4. Ryan
5. James
6. Callum
7. Andrew
8. Dylan
9. Ross
10. Jamie
11. Matthew
12. Adam
13. Daniel
14. Liam
15. Scott
16. Connor
17. Kieran
18. David
19. Jordan
20. Kyle
21. Michael
22. Ben
23. Thomas
24. John
25. Aidan
26. Criag
27. Sean
28. Alexander
29. Nathan
30. Joshua
31. Calum
32. Robbie
33. William
34. Luke
35. Euan
36. Declan
37. Aaron
38. Ewan
39. Christopher
40. Reece
41. Robert
42. Fraser
43. Josh
44. Mark
45. Ethan
46. Paul
47. Brandon
48. Jay
49. Samuel
50. Finlay

Other Books on

GENERAL BOOKS

1. Child Development **(New)**
2. Abraham Lincoln : A Complete Biography **(New)**
3. Mein Kampf : My Struggle **(New)**
4. Think & Grow Rich **(New)**
5. The Art of Personality Development **(New)**
6. Positive Mind Power (New)
7. Travel & Tourism An Industry Facilitator (New)
8. World's Great Authors And Poets (New)
9. Judgment No Aircrash No Death (New)
10. Effective Editing Help Yourself in Becoming A Good Editor (New)
11. Smart House-Keeping for Modern Women
12. Develop Super Power Memory
13. World's Great Personalities
14. Personality Plus
15. Power of Positive Thinking
16. Art of Successful Parenting
17. A Handbook of Etiquettes
18. How to Beat Your Competitors
19. How to Negotiate Effectively
20. World's Great Scientists
21. Patriot The Unique Indian Leader Netaji Subhas Chandra Bose
22. Body Language
23. Art of Successful Living
24. Make Your Boss Happy

24. Jokes for All
25. Selected Dohas
26. Baby Names for Girls (New)
27. Baby Names for Boys (New)
28. Art of Public Speaking
29. The World's Greatest Speeches
30. Group Discussions
31. Personality Development
32. Think Positive & Things Will Go Right
33. Once in a Blue Moon (A Tantra Tale)
34. God is Dead
35. Travel India (A Complete Guide For Tourists)
36. Glimpses of Urdu Poetry
37. Indian Mythology
38. Helpline for Stressed Parents
39. Grow Rich with Peace of Mind
40. How to be Fit & Young (New)
41. How to Succeed in Life
42. How to Reduce Tension
43. A Book of Stenography
44. Business Letters
45. Baby Names for the Boy
46. Baby Names for the Girl
47. Non Vegetarian Delights
48. Pure Vegetarian Delights

Lotus PRESS

Unit No. 220, Second Floor, 4735/22,
Prakash Deep Building, Ansari Road, Darya Ganj,
New Delhi - 110002, Ph.: ~~32903912~~, 23280047, 09811594448
E-mail: lotuspress1984@gmail.com, www.lotuspress.co.in